A BRIEF HISTORY OF

The First
Thousand Years

A BRIEF HISTORY OF THE CATHOLIC CHURCH IN CANADA

The First Thousand Years

Raymond J. Lahey

NOVALIS

NOVALIS

© 2002 Novalis, Saint Paul University, Ottawa, Canada

Cover: John Lee, Heidy Lawrance Associates
Layout: Heidy Lawrance Associates
Editor: Bernadette Gasslein

Front Cover

TOP LEFT: Madre Bernarda—Courtesy Soeurs de la Providence, Québec.

BOTTOM LEFT: Kateri Tekakwitha—Courtesy of and © 1986 Robert Lentz. Color reproductions
               available from Bridge Building Images • 1-802-864-8346 • *www.BridgeBuilding.com*

TOP RIGHT: Bishop François de Laval—Courtesy Centre d'animation François-de-Laval, Québec.

BOTTOM RIGHT: World Youth Day 2002/Journée mondiale de la jeunesse 2002, Toronto—
               © Bill Wittman.

Back Cover

TOP: Scottish immigrants on a train...ca 1911. William Topley, National Archives of
               Canada, PA-008497.

BOTTOM: Galician immigrant family. National Archives of Canada, C-004745.

Business Office:
Novalis
49 Front Street East, 2nd Floor
Toronto, Ontario, Canada
M5E 1B3

Phone: 1-800-387-7164 or (416) 363-3303
Fax: 1-800-204-4140 or (416) 363-9409
E-mail: *cservice@novalis.ca*

National Library of Canada Cataloguing in Publication Data

Lahey, Raymond J.
   The first thousand years : a brief history of the Catholic Church
in Canada / Raymond J. Lahey.

ISBN 2-89507-235-3

   1. Catholic Church—Canada—History. I. Title.

BX1421.3.L33 2002   282'.71   C2002-901621-5

Printed in Canada.

We acknowledge the financial support of the Government of Canada through the Book Publishing
Industry Development Program (BPIDP) for our publishing activities.

Page 21: "Brébeuf and his Brethren" by E.J. Pratt was originally published as *Brébeuf and his
Brethren: The North American Martyrs*. Basilian Press, 1942; [Toronto]: Macmillan of Canada,
[c1966].

10 9 8 7 6 5 4 3 2 1   10 09 08 07 06 05 04 03 02

Contents

Introduction

THE HISTORY OF the Church is never simply a history of buildings and bishops. At the deeper level it is the story of passing on the flame of faith from one generation to the next, and of the people who carried that torch and kept aglow its light. For at its heart, the Church is not an organization or an institution, but a communion of persons. The hopes people lived by and the choices they made affected not only people of their own day, but also future generations. These hopes, these choices, are the threads that form the fabric of this history.

Such a short history can only introduce the Church in Canada to Canadians and to others. In writing it, I have been struck by both the Church's breadth, in every sense of that word, and by its energy and vitality. I am even more aware of how much I have had to omit: of the many events and movements not recorded here, of the numerous Canadians whose faith and love contributed so much to those around them and who are passed by in silence.

This book is dedicated to our Canadian ancestors in the faith—not just those whose names appear here, or on the pages of any written history, but to all those young people and elders from every race and nation who in so many different ways gave witness to the Gospel, and from whom we have received so great a treasure. We can say of them what the French version of "O Canada" says: *"Il sait porter la croix"* – "You knew how to carry the cross." From them we have received it, that we too might hold it high and treasure the Christian legacy they have passed on to us. For this, to all of them, we can only be humbly grateful.

Raymond J. Lahey
Bishop of St. George's

1

America's First Christians:
The Vikings

TODAY WE KNOW that the sixth-century Irish monk St. Brendan the Navigator sailed far and wide in the North Atlantic using a *curragh*, a small frame boat covered with hides. His tale is told in the medieval document *The Voyage of St. Brendan the Abbot*, but it is hard to reconcile its sometimes mythic descriptions with particular places. Many believe that using other islands as stepping stones Brendan reached North America, and a few years ago such a voyage was actually duplicated. However, firm evidence of this does not exist.

The first known European settlers in Canada, and America's first Christians, were the Norse, or the Vikings. We know now that Norse had sailed as far as Canada before the year 1000, and that some Christian Norse settled here around that date. One of their settlements, at L'Anse aux Meadows on the northern tip of Newfoundland, has now been excavated.

Probably the first Norse explorer to sight the coast of Canada was the Icelander Bjarni Herjolfsson in 986, but the real story of Christian settlement begins with the voyage of Leifr Eiriksson in the year 1000. Leifr (often called "the Lucky") was the son of Eirik Thorvaldsson ("Eiric the Red"), who colonized western Greenland. Like many Norse Eirik was pagan, but Leifr had gone to the court of the Norwegian King, Olaf Tryggvason (995-1000), where he became a Christian. When the king learned Leifr was returning home, he told him: "You are to go there with a mission from me: to preach Christianity in Greenland." With this intention, Leifr and his companions sailed from Norway, but driven off course they came instead to the western lands, first "Helluland" ("slab-land," Baffin Island), and then "Markland" ("forest-land," Labrador). Two days sail later they reached a place where, either on that first voyage or on a return voyage soon afterwards, they built houses and settled for the winter season. The location of their colony is not certain, but its physical description closely matches the L'Anse aux Meadows settlement. Leifr himself stayed there only one winter before returning to Greenland. There he was true to his promise to King Olaf, "preaching Christianity and the Catholic faith throughout the country."

A few years later, a second expedition was organized by Leifr's brother, Thorvald, and a party of thirty, who reoccupied Leifr's old settlement. The group stayed there two years, but Thorvald himself was killed in fighting with the *skraelings* (possibly Inuit). The story of his burial recounts the first planting of the cross on the soil of

America. Knowing he was dying, Thorvald asked to be taken to a headland he had named "*Kjalarness.*" "Bury me there," was his request, "and put crosses at my head and feet, and let the place be called *Krossaness* for ever afterwards." The exact location of this site is uncertain, but it is likely near Cape Porcupine in Labrador.

A third settlement occurred around the year 1010, and was led by Thorfinnr Thordarson (known as Karlsefni) and his wife Gutrid, the widow of another of Leifr Eiriksson's brothers. With them was a considerably larger group of Norse that included some who were Christian and some who were still pagan, and a Scottish couple, 160 people in all. They settled at a place they called "Straumfjord" ("current-fjord," possibly somewhere on the Gulf of

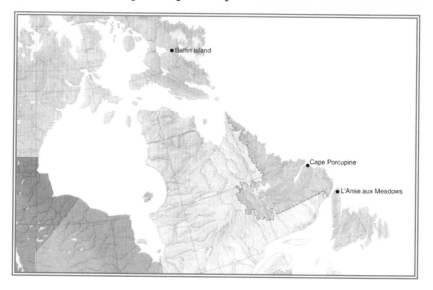

St. Lawrence) where they lived for three years, and where a son, Snorri, was born to Thorfinnr and Gutrid. The account of this expedition specifically records the first known baptisms in America, those of two *skraeling* boys whom the Norse had captured, probably in Labrador, and whom the Norse seem to have accepted into their own community.

Thereafter there are no clear accounts that the Norse continued to settle in America. One of the few intriguing records we have is a short note from 1121 A.D. about Bishop Eirikr Gnupsson, then a missionary bishop for the western Norse lands. It says only that "Bishop Eirikr from Greenland went to look for Vinland." Of his intentions, or the outcome of his voyage, we know nothing. Somewhat later Father Ivar Bardarson, administrator of the diocese of Gadar, Greenland from about 1340 to 1360, directly or indirectly acquired solid information about the eastern Canadian Arctic, but whether he personally visited there is not known. As late as 1347 the Norse made a voyage from Greenland to Labrador, and there is considerable evidence of sustained contact between the Norse and the Inuit. However by the late middle ages, even the Norse colonies in Greenland had disappeared, and it would be people of other nations who would bring back to Canada the cross that the Norse had first planted.

2

Replanting the Cross:
Seafarers and Explorers

CHRISTOPHER COLUMBUS' voyage to the Caribbean in 1492 is the first clearly established post-Norse voyage to the New World. However, other European explorers may have preceded Columbus. Portuguese sailors were actively engaged in the exploration of the Atlantic well before 1492, and some historians would suggest that they reached the American continent. A letter from an Englishman, John Day, written in 1497 or 1498, probably to Columbus, suggests that the land just discovered by John Cabot (Giovanni Caboto), an Italian explorer sailing from England, was the same land that sailors from Bristol in England had found some time before. Expeditions from Bristol definitely had probed the North Atlantic as early as 1480-81, and perhaps again in the early 1490s, but whether they reached the American landmass is uncertain.

Whatever the other claims, the first of these European explorers known to have reached Canada was Cabot, a citizen of Venice. After an unsuccessful voyage a year earlier, in May 1497 he sailed from Bristol with authority from the English king, Henry VII. He followed a straight course from southern Ireland, and made his landfall 35 days later, on June 24. Near that same place Cabot went ashore "with a crucifix," and "raised banners bearing the arms of the Holy Father and the arms of the King of England." For about a month he explored the coastline, seeing signs of habitation but no Natives, and then returned to England. Where Cabot landed is disputed—anywhere from southern Nova Scotia to northern Newfoundland—although a straight course from Ireland would have brought him closer to the latter. But Cabot's voyage, and his carrying the cross ashore certainly marked a new era from which the Christian presence in Canada today can trace its roots.

No priests seem to have accompanied Cabot on this first voyage to Canada. However, on a further trip the next year two clerics, Father Giovanni Antonio de Carbonariis from Milan, and a Spanish friar named Buil, who had sailed previously with Columbus, went with him. Cabot's purpose was to found a colony, but his voyage ended in disaster. Details are scarce, but one of his ships (with Father Buil aboard) returned to Ireland early, and four others were lost. Whether Cabot reached Canada again is unknown, as is the fate of Father de Carbonariis.

But Cabot's voyages prompted further exploration. From 1500 Portuguese seamen, especially the brothers Gaspar and Miguel Corte-Real, and João Fernandez (who perhaps named Labrador), became avid explorers of North

America, and their observations led to the first maps of Canada. Several English expeditions visited Newfoundland between 1501 and 1505. By 1504 the French were fishing off Newfoundland, and two years later Portugal imposed a tax on fish caught there. Trade grew quickly. By 1527, when the Englishman John Rut visited St. John's, Newfoundland, he found there 14 fishing ships: 12 French, and 2 Portuguese.

With Rut was a priest, Albertus de Prato. An unnamed priest had also sailed to Newfoundland with the English merchant Hugh Eliot in 1504. Indeed, there is much to indicate that the presence of clergy on these exploratory voyages was commonplace. The seamen of that era were often devout men who understood the dangers they faced

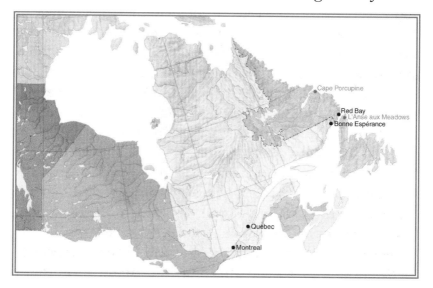

and, even without clergy, prayed together as a normal part of their daily shipboard life.

Although exploration advanced quickly, settlement did not. Thomas Aubert of Dieppe in France may have tried to found a Newfoundland colony about 1508. Again, the Portuguese adventurer João Alvares Fagundes, who explored Nova Scotia and southern Newfoundland in 1521, later appears to have organized a permanent shore establishment with colonists from Portugal and the Azores, perhaps on Cape Breton. However his little colony encountered many difficulties, and probably did not last more than two years.

The detailed exploration of the St. Lawrence basin, including western Newfoundland, Prince Edward Island, and part of New Brunswick, belongs to the 1534 voyage of Jacques Cartier, from Saint-Malo, France. To express both the faith and French territorial claims, Cartier also planted the cross, actually three times, first on the lower North Shore of the St. Lawrence, then in the Magdalene Islands, and finally on the Gaspé peninsula. On that voyage we also have the earliest recorded Mass in Canada, celebrated on June 11, 1534 (St. Barnabas Day) at the harbour called Brest (Bonne Espérance near St. Paul's River), Quebec. On a second voyage in 1535, Cartier went as far as Quebec City and Montreal (Mont-Royal), applying to the region the term Canada, the Native name for the Quebec area.

Perhaps the most remarkable early Catholic presence in Canada was in the thriving and semi-permanent

Basque settlement near Red Bay, Labrador, on the Straits of Belle-Isle. These whaling stations began in the 1540s and continued for about fifty years. Whether priests were regularly assigned there is not clear, but they were sometimes among the company, and one of the graves found there may belong to a priest. While the whalers usually stayed from May to December, sometimes they had to over-winter there, often unprepared. Indeed, one of the most striking testimonies of that era is a will the whaler Joanes de Echaniz wrote on Christmas Eve, 1584, just before he died in Labrador entrusting his soul to Jesus Christ, "believing as I do believe in all that the Holy Roman Catholic Church maintains and believes." His simple faith probably voiced the prayer of many of the first Europeans to be buried in Canadian soil.

3

Membertou:
Chief and Christian

AS EUROPEAN CONTACT with Canada became frequent, so did encounters with its aboriginal peoples. Some may have been well intentioned. Perhaps it was persuasion that induced three Innu from Newfoundland (probably Beothuk) to return to England with Bristol merchants in 1502. Presented to Henry VII, they remained for some years at the English court. Thomas Aubert may have done likewise in 1508, when he took to France seven Native people with their canoes and other artifacts. Other actions were clearly hostile. In 1501 Gaspar Corte-Real had captured 57 Natives, again likely Beothuk, whom he brought back to Portugal as slaves. But not all contact was so aggressive; indeed the Montagnais worked with the Basques in the whaling industry.

Although many official sixteenth-century documents about Canada included high-sounding words about Christianizing non-Christian lands, there was no real effort to bring the Gospel to the aboriginal peoples of Canada. In fact, there was surprisingly little interest in them generally, and European accounts of Canada in this period provide only superficial descriptions of Native life.

European settlement and the development of a fur trade with the Native peoples changed things quickly. In 1607, at the first Acadian settlement at Port-Royal, Nova Scotia (begun in 1604 at Ile Sainte-Croix, Maine, but moved the next year), the lieutenant-governor, Jean de Poutrincourt, earnestly tried to establish just and friendly relations with the local Mi'kmaq, and the lawyer Marc Lescarbot gave them weekly religious instruction. Indeed, Lescarbot maintained a keen interest in Canada's Native peoples, and later published much about their way of life.

The French had to abandon Port-Royal for two years, but accompanied by the secular priest, Jessé Fléché, they returned in 1610 with a clear mission to bring Christianity to the Natives. Here on June 24, Father Fléché baptized the warrior Membertou, chief of the local Mi'kmaqs, with his wife and twenty of his family. Membertou, who took the Christian name Henri, was thus the first aboriginal person to receive solemn baptism in Canada.

Membertou, although sometimes ignorant of Christian doctrine, was a sincere convert. He renounced the practices of shamanism and polygamy, and tried to conform to Catholic traditions. He urged the three missionaries there (Jesuit Fathers Pierre Biard and Enémond Massé had arrived in 1611) to learn Mi'kmaq so that he could deepen his catechesis. Unfortunately, Membertou, who by some accounts was over 100, died on September 18 that year.

Taking his faith seriously to the end, he confessed his sins, was anointed, and changed his original wish to be buried with his ancestors to seek burial in consecrated ground.

Membertou's acceptance of Catholicism marked a turning point. In small groups at first (about 100 in 1610-11), but in ever-increasing numbers, many of the Mi'kmaq people followed his step. By the time of the famed Father Pierre Maillard, who lived among them from 1735 to 1762, virtually the whole Mi'kmaq nation had become Catholic. Further, Membertou's encouragement contributed to a true missionary spirit. Fathers Biard and Massé and their successors viewed their mission to the Natives as their sacred duty. They made every effort to learn the language, and even succeeded in producing a small phonetic catechism. Similar

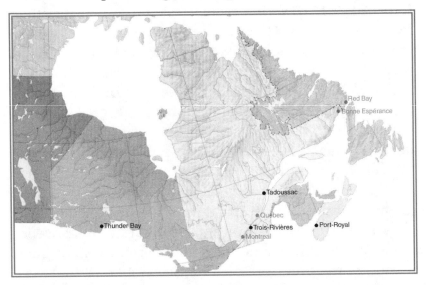

work was done by Récollect (Franciscan) Father Chrestien Le Clerq among the Mi'kmaq of Gaspé and the Miramachi between 1675 and 1686, and later by Father Maillard, who eventually codified the written Mi'kmaq language and trained literate Native catechists. The French policy of friendship toward the Mi'kmaq and the commercial ties of the fur trade obviously supported this missionary activity.

The mission among the Mi'kmaq was the forerunner of Récollect and Jesuit efforts to evangelize Canada's Native peoples. With the arrival of the Récollect order in 1615, Father Jean Dolbeau began to minister among the Montagnais at Tadoussac on the lower St. Lawrence. His colleague Joseph Le Caron established the first mission among the Hurons at Carhagoua near Thunder Bay, where on August 12 he celebrated the first Mass in present-day Ontario. Brother Pacifique Duplessis preached the Gospel and cared for the Algonkins around Trois-Rivières. The efforts of the Récollects to be present to the aboriginal peoples and to understand their ways were heroic; the hardships they endured were incredible. Father Guillaume Poulain was captured and tortured by the Iroquois in 1622, but escaped and continued on his mission. Father Nicholas Viel, murdered near Montreal in 1625 during a mission among the Hurons, is often considered the first Canadian martyr. Although politics caused the eventual exclusion of the Récollects from New France in 1632, Jesuits had by then taken up their Huron and Montagnais missions. It was a case of heroism built on heroism.

Early European Settlers: "Many crosses and little bread"

COMMERCE, NOT colonization, governed European attitudes to Canada in the 1500s. Profits from fish and fur, and the prospect of a passage through Canada to China were the dominant factors. Projects for Canadian settlements sometimes surfaced, but nothing concrete came of them.

Religion often lurked behind such proposals, for Canada was seen as a haven for persecuted minorities. Thus English Catholic backers supported Sir Humphrey Gilbert's attempt to establish a Newfoundland colony in the 1580s, while the impetus for French colonization came largely from Huguenots. Indeed, a major reason for the long delay in French settlement in Canada was the assassination of the Protestant leadership on St. Bartholomew's Day, 1572.

Things changed quickly toward the turn of the century, but these first attempts were short-lived. The nobleman Trolius de la Roche established a colony of "vagabonds and beggars" on Sable Island, Nova Scotia, in 1598. It survived, despite difficulties, until 1603. Similarly, in 1600, the Calvinist military officer Pierre de Chauvin began an outpost at the fur-trading center of Tadoussac, but the first winter there was disastrous enough to end the venture.

Permanent settlement in Canada had to await the foundation of Port-Royal in 1605 and Quebec in 1608. Planned as a base for the fur trade, Port-Royal was settled by Pierre Du Gua de Monts, a Huguenot, with a mixed group of artisans and adventurers, Catholics and Protestants. Its first company included two priests and a Huguenot minister. One of the priests, Nicholas Aubry, left soon after his arrival. The second, whose name is unknown, perhaps Canada's first resident priest, succumbed to scurvy during the winter of 1605-6. The colony's backers sent Father Fleché as a replacement

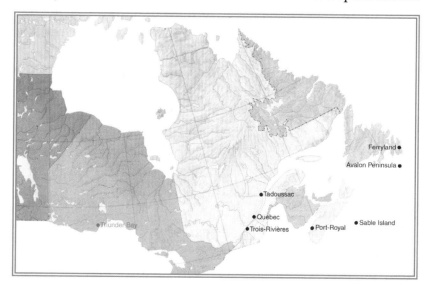

in 1610, but anxious about its Catholicity, the King entrusted Acadia to the Jesuits. A wealthy patroness had assigned half the colony's profits to support them, but when profits did not materialize, sharp disputes arose between the Jesuits and Port-Royal's leaders. The Jesuits left in 1613, just before Acadia suffered the first of several English attempts to destroy it.

With the founding of Quebec, French interest shifted from Acadia to the St. Lawrence River. Like Port-Royal, Quebec was founded by de Monts, who put it under the direction of the explorer Samuel de Champlain. Built at the narrows of the St. Lawrence, it was first just a trading post for furs, and began to take on a settled character only with the arrival of the Récollects in 1615. They saw it as both a base for their Native missions and a centre for ministering to the French colonists, who in the words of one of them, "had many crosses and little bread."

By 1621, the Récollects had built a monastery, Our Lady of the Angels, and had priests serving the posts at Trois-Rivières and Tadoussac. They farmed the land, operated a school for Native children, and staffed a mission to the Hurons 800 miles to the west. But such demands rapidly became too heavy for them alone, and led them to request assistance from the Jesuits, who arrived at Quebec in 1625.

Quebec still lived a fragile existence. In 1629, the English captured it and deported the missionaries to France, thus dealing a real blow to the religious presence. Not until 1633 did missionaries return. Only the Jesuits came back; for political reasons the Récollects were excluded from the colony to which they had contributed so much.

By then Britain had several Canadian settlements; the first was at Cupids, Newfoundland, in 1610. All were settled largely by Protestants. An exception was the Newfoundland colony that Sir George Calvert (Lord Baltimore) established in 1621 at Ferryland. He named it Avalon, after the first foundation of Christianity in Britain. In 1625, Calvert resigned as Principal Secretary to the King, and declared his Catholicism. He sent a Catholic governor and a party of 15 Catholic settlers to the colony. On a visit in 1627, he brought with him two priests, including Father Anthony Pole (alias "Smith"), who became the first resident English priest in Canada, staying there for two years. In 1628-9, Baltimore himself settled there with his wife and family, a group of Catholics, and additional priests, but disagreeable weather led him to transfer his attentions south to what became Maryland. His Avalon colony is particularly notable because, like Port-Royal, it clearly attempted, with both Catholic and Anglican clergy and settlers, to introduce religious toleration to the New World. It would be long before that ideal became the norm.

5

Blackrobe Martyrs:
Brébeuf and his Brethren

IN THE STORY OF the Canadian Church, the Jesuit mission among the Hurons (Wendat) holds a singular place. Jesuits had served in Acadia from 1611 to 1613, and responded readily when the Récollets in Quebec invited their assistance in 1625. The following year two Jesuit priests, including the young Jean de Brébeuf, were assigned to the Huron territory. This one month and 800-mile journey to the west by canoe brought the missionaries to a people who by then had become close allies of the French. Brébeuf spent three years among them but achieved little; in 1629, the English capture of Quebec forced his return to France.

Back in Canada in 1633 and encouraged by his Jesuit superior, Father Paul Le Jeune, Brébeuf launched a new and more organized mission in the Georgian Bay area. He and his fellow Jesuits ("Blackrobes," or "those called charcoal" to the Huron, from their black cassocks) gradually mastered the language and adapted to the life of the Native people. However, evangelization soon met with growing opposition, which Brébeuf attributed to three factors: immorality, Native traditions, and the devastating effect of European diseases that had killed 60% of the Huron nation. So strong ran the feelings and threats of violence against the Jesuits, that in 1637 Brébeuf feared for their lives, but could still write to his superiors: "Whatever may happen, I can assure you that all our Fathers await the outcome of this affair with calm and untroubled spirits." In 1640 Brébeuf and a companion were beaten. By 1641, when a broken clavicle obliged him to go to Quebec, there were less than 100 Christians.

From a distance, Brébeuf acted as procurator for the Huron mission for three years; there he wrote the "Huron Carol." Finally, in 1644 he was able to return. He entered into a storm. The Iroquois, sensing the weakness of the Hurons, their traditional enemies, and seeking to replace them in the fur trade, had begun a campaign of genocide. From 1642 they made their attacks on a wide front. That year, Father Isaac Jogues and two Jesuit *donnés* (lay associates) were captured and severely tortured. On September 29, René Goupil, who had made his vows as a lay brother in captivity, became the first Jesuit martyr when an angry Iroquois killed him, apparently for making the sign of the cross over a child. Jogues and the other *donné* were eventually released. In 1644, an Italian Jesuit, Francesco-Giuseppe Bressani, was similarly captured and tortured. Despite his treatment, Jogues returned twice to the Iroquois as an emissary, but in 1646 he was received with hostility, and he and his companion, a young *donné* named Jean La Lande, were both murdered by hatchet blows.

In 1648 the Iroquois attacks increased in ferocity. Father Antoine Daniel was shot to death trying to save his people; 700 of them were taken prisoner. The next spring saw new attacks. Fathers Brébeuf and Gabriel Lalemant, refusing to flee, were taken prisoner and horribly martyred on March 16-17, between Coldwater and Vasey, Ontario. Later that year Father Charles Garnier, missionary to the Tobacco Nation (Petuns), was slaughtered outside his chapel, and Father Noël Chabanel, who remained among the Hurons despite his struggles with their language, was killed by a Huron apostate. Even in 1655 Mohawks killed Brother Jean Liègeois at Sillery, near Quebec.

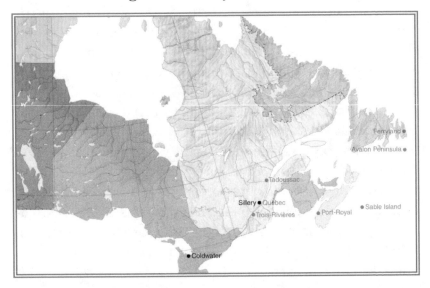

Decimated by the Iroquois attacks, the once great Huron confederacy was destroyed. The remaining Jesuits had no alternative but to leave their mission and try to rescue the remnant of the Huron people. In 1650, Father Paul Ragneau, the Jesuit superior, led a group of 300 survivors back to Quebec.

Paradoxically, these terrible trials led to a new spring of conversions, with 3,000 baptisms recorded in 1649-50 alone. And the Huron Christians who were dispersed among the other Native peoples and prisoners of the Iroquois often became a nucleus for the further spread of Christianity.

In 1930, Pope Pius XI canonized Fathers Brébeuf, Jogues, Daniel, Garnier, Chabanel and Lalemant, Brother Goupil, and the layman La Lande as martyrs for the faith. Perhaps the epitaph for their mission is the epic poem "Brébeuf and his Brethren" by the renowned Canadian poet E.J. Pratt:

> But even from there was the old tale retold
> Of hunger and the search for roots and acorns
> Of cold and persecution unto death
> By the Iroquois; of Jesuit will and courage ...

6

Saints among the Native Peoples: Joseph Chihwatenha and Kateri Tekakwitha

NATIVE CHRISTIANS equaled the missionaries in heroism. One of the early converts was Chihwatenha, baptized Joseph, a Huron from Ossossanë, in the Georgian Bay region. From the arrival of the Jesuits, Chihwatenha listened attentively to their teachings and on August 16, 1637, during a bout of serious illness, he was baptized. His wife, Marie Aonetta, two nieces, and a nephew received baptism soon afterwards, and for a while were the only Christian family in his village.

Joseph Chihwatenha was an exemplary Christian, assisting the Jesuits in their mission work, defending them against criticism, professing his faith publicly, and encouraging his people to adopt Christianity. This he did at real danger to himself, for the Jesuits were often considered sorcerers, but his was a sure faith in God. "I have with me and for me the One who is all powerful," he had told his people. On August 2, 1640, while alone just outside his village, he was murdered, perhaps by Iroquois raiders, but more likely by Huron opponents of his faith. Blessed Marie de l'Incarnation called him "an apostle with apostles."

Chihwatenha's faith lived on. Aonetta, his wife, continued his efforts. Three days after Chihwatenha's death, his brother, Teondechoren, a cult-healer who had resisted Christianity, sought baptism, and, also taking the name Joseph, became a fervent convert. A niece, Theresa Oionhaton, who stayed for two years with the Ursulines in Quebec, preached the Gospel to her people, even as a teenager. Captured by the Iroquois in 1642, she held to her faith and her prayer life; in 1654, still in captivity, she rejoiced at making a new convert. Such was Chihwatenha's legacy.

The Jesuit *Relations* tell of many captured Hurons who, like Theresa, remained faithful Christians. They speak of those who asked only to pray before being put to death, and who could say to their torturers, as one did: "I am going to Heaven, where I will pray to him who has made all for your salvation." Others tried to catechize their Iroquois captors. Their example made a lasting impression.

By the 1650s, the Jesuits had made contact with several Native nations. These included Mi'kmaq from Cape Breton to Gaspé, Montagnais and Algonkians along the St. Lawrence, Ottawas [Odawas] on the upper Great Lakes, Neutrals on the Niagara peninsula, Petuns on the Bruce peninsula, and Nipissings. In 1654, amidst an uneasy truce, a request for missionaries arrived from the Onondagas, one of the Iroquois Five Nations. Father Simon

Le Moyne and others made several trips into Iroquois territory, both Onondaga and Mohawk, between then and 1661. These trips encouraged the Christian prisoners; they also paved the way for peace.

A formal Iroquois mission begun in 1657 lasted just a year, but ten years later, when peace was made with the Mohawks, a new request came for missionaries. The first group of three Jesuit priests and two associates were cared for in the village of Gandaouagué by a young girl named Tekakwitha, who was much impressed by them. She had been born to a Christian Algonkin mother and a Mohawk father, but both were killed by smallpox, which left her pock-marked and partly blind. Over time, Tekakwitha increased her knowledge of Christianity from the

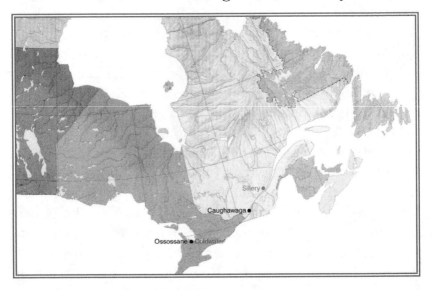

many Hurons and Algonkians in her village. Finally at age 20 she sought baptism, which she received on Easter, 1676, taking the name Kateri.

Almost immediately Kateri was persecuted for her beliefs. Because she refused to work on Sundays, she was deprived of food; she even received death threats. Eventually she left her own village and made her way to Caughnawaga, a Christian community near Montreal. Here, with her mother's friend, Anastasie Tegonhatsiongo, as her spiritual guide, she practiced a life of mortification and prayer. She considered founding a community of Native sisters, and she herself took a vow of perpetual chastity. She died in 1680, just 24, and almost immediately became regarded as a saint.

In time many Iroquois became Catholics, although often in the face of opposition from their own people. But the Iroquois also had some outstanding Christian leaders, including Onondaga chief Daniel Garakontié, baptized in the cathedral of Quebec in 1669. He led an exemplary life, assisted the missionaries, and promoted peace. Similarly, chief Joseph Togouiroui, the "Great Mohawk," became a convert in 1673, settling at the mission village with 40 of his friends. Year after year he led others to the faith. After his death in 1690, one account said: "the missionaries were those who felt this loss most cruelly." In less than forty years heroism, both Native and missionary, had accomplished remarkable things.

7

The "City of Mary": Jeanne Mance and Marguerite Bourgeoys

THE FOUNDING OF Montreal was a religious undertaking: a base for Catholicism in New France, conceived by a French lay mystic, Jerome Le Royer de La Dauversière, and supported by a pious foundation, the Société Notre-Dame de Montréal. The details of the project were entrusted to a 29-year-old soldier, Paul de Chomedey de Maisonneuve. On May 17, 1642, at the foot of Mount Royal, Maisonneuve and his colonists solemnly founded the settlement they called "Ville-Marie," "City of Mary."

The party numbered about 50 men and four women. Construction was their first priority, and by the next year they had a fort, a chapel, lodging for 70 people, and a hospital. The nature of the colony was aptly recorded in 1643: "The inhabitants live for the most part communally, as in a sort of inn; others live on their private means, but all live in Jesus Christ, with one heart and soul."

The next quarter-century would be for them a time of unceasing struggle against both hardship and Iroquois ambushes. Often settlers would be picked off one by one, six in one day alone in 1643. In 1651, the settlement almost fell to the constant attacks. Over the years, only Maisonneuve's inspired leadership ensured its survival.

The founder of the hospital (Hôtel-Dieu) and the bursar for the colony was Jeanne Mance, a 36-year-old single woman, who had nursed the wounded in France. A deeply spiritual person, she came to Canada because she believed this was God's will for her. Aided by a French benefactress, she was able to construct a proper hospital in 1645; it was she who provided capital for Maisonneuve to hire sufficient soldiers to defend the colony. In 1659, she was responsible for bringing to Montreal three religious Hospitallers of St. Joseph; these sisters put on a firm foundation her work of caring for the sick, both French and Native.

Montreal was first served by Jesuits, but M. Olier, the founder of the Sulpicians, had been actively involved in the Société de Montréal, and in 1657 sent a group of his priests there, under the Abbé Gabriel Thubières de Levy de Queylus. They became the parish clergy of the island, and from the beginning were deeply involved in its affairs, religious and civic. Their involvement deepened after 1663, when the Société, which owned most of the island, ceded it to the seminary the Sulpicians had established. They did much to promote colonization, and saw the population of the settlement grow to almost 1500 by 1671.

Within two months in 1661, two Sulpicians, Jacques Le Maistre and Guillaume Vignal, had lost their lives to the Iroquois, but that did not prevent the Sulpicians from launching their own Native missions. By 1670 they had three missions on Lake Ontario, where they served amid great difficulties until 1680, when their superior ordered them to abandon those missions and concentrate their efforts on the missions nearer Montreal.

Early Montreal held many remarkable persons, perhaps none more so than Marguerite Bourgeoys. In 1653, at the age of 33, she had volunteered her services to Maisonneuve for the education of the young. She was unable to begin a school until 1658, when she took her first pupils in a converted stable, and the next year she brought other young women back from France to help her. These women came to be regarded as "sisters," but they lacked official status, so in 1670, Marguerite went to Paris alone to see the King and obtain his permission. When he granted it a year later, the King noted that she had offered free education, prepared girls to earn a livelihood, constructed buildings, cleared land, and set up a farm.

Her "filles de la Congrégation" were secular sisters who responded to the needs of the times. Marguerite's realism and spirituality guided them. The sisters must be "wanderers and not cloistered," she wrote, so that they could go where the poor were. Thus they had a great impact throughout New France, especially in the education of less privileged women, including Native women.

Marguerite Bourgeoys' last years were occupied with seeking formal church acknowledgement as religious for her sisters. This finally came in 1698, when the almost 40 sisters were recognized as the Congrégation de Notre-Dame. Marguerite herself died two years later, regarded even then as a saint. St. Marguerite Bourgeoys was canonized in 1982.

8

The Apostle of Canada:
François de Laval

CANADA LONG LACKED proper church organization. Historically the Archbishop of Rouen in France had claimed jurisdiction, and in 1649 he appointed the Jesuit superior in Quebec as vicar-general for New France. Unfortunately he did the same in 1657 for Abbé de Queylus, the Sulpician superior. Disputes arose quickly, and in 1658 the Archbishop limited Queylus' jurisdiction to Montreal.

This was only a beginning. A bishop for Quebec was being considered; the French clergy proposed Queylus. The Jesuits quietly promoted instead a former student, François de Laval. Rome hesitated, but then appointed Laval vicar-apostolic (directly subject to Rome), not a titular bishop.The Archbishop of Rouen was outraged, and tried to prevent his consecration, but on December 8, 1658, Laval was secretly consecrated by the papal nuncio. The Archbishop had the Rouen *parlement* forbid the King's subjects to acknowledge Laval as vicar-apostolic. In turn, the Queen-regent had to write the governor in Quebec that only Laval's authority should be recognized there.

Canada's first bishop reached Quebec on June 16, 1659. He was 36, a former archdeacon who had devoted himself to the sick, the young, and the poor. Always attracted to the missions, he was to have gone in 1652 to Tonkin (Vietnam) as vicar-apostolic, but the project did not proceed. In 1654 he had resigned as archdeacon and entered a life of prayer and charity at the Hermitage in Caen, a city in Normandy, northern France.

Throughout the dispute over his appointment Laval remained silent. However, once in Canada he firmly asserted his episcopal authority. He likewise asserted his independence from the state by putting clerical discipline under church courts, and by rejecting the governor's precedence in the liturgy.

Laval's great objective was to establish a diocesan clergy and provide for their support. Thus he founded a seminary that would not only offer theological education, but by receiving the church tithes would be able to appoint and support parish clergy. His scheme was criticized, but it worked, and although he eventually had to establish autonomous parishes, the seminary often had to subsidize them. Laval's promotion of a settled diocesan clergy made a lasting contribution to the enculturation of the church in Canadian society.

He often battled the authorities, especially over the supply of liquor to the Natives, which he loathed, but which profited the merchants. In the end Laval achieved partial success, but not the total ban he wanted. Here he was sometimes undermined by the Récollects, who had been reintroduced to Canada in 1670, supposedly to counter the severity of the bishop and the Jesuits.

To avoid questions about authority, Laval sought the establishment of a regular diocese. Accordingly, on October 1, 1674, Pope Clement X formally constituted most of North America as the Diocese of Quebec. (Quebec is thus Canada's first, or primatial, see, and its Archbishop the Primate of Canada.) Laval's other concern was for a successor, since after an illness in 1681 he found the work exhausting. He himself selected Abbé Saint-Vallier, a French secular priest from the nobility, who went to Quebec in 1685 as vicar-general. When Saint-Vallier (only 34) was ordained bishop in 1688, Laval resigned. He left a

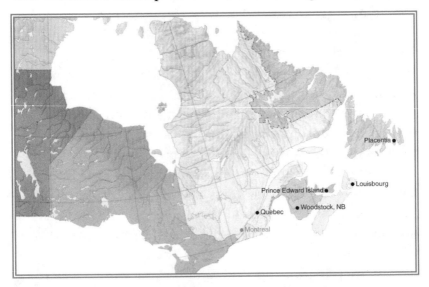

thriving diocese; there were now 24 parishes, 102 priests (13 Canadian born), and 97 sisters.

Laval himself was extraordinary. He prayed constantly, worked slavishly, and lived frugally, literally giving everything to the poor. Even during his lifetime Marie de l'Incarnation wrote: "I do not say that he is a saint, that would be saying too much; but I will truthfully say that he lives like a saint and an apostle." Laval remained in retirement until his death in 1708; in 1980, the Church declared him Blessed.

Unfortunately, his successor, Saint-Vallier, immediately became embroiled in a quarrel with the seminary that completely divided the diocese and made his effective leadership impossible. By 1694, almost the whole diocese opposed him. Constant controversies and five years of British captivity kept him absent from Quebec from 1694 until 1713, except for the years 1697-1700. But his accomplishments were real, especially the growth of the church in the remote areas of the diocese. As vicar-general he had established a mission near Woodstock, New Brunswick in 1686; as a new bishop, a parish at Placentia, Newfoundland in 1689; a parish at Louisbourg, Cape Breton in 1714 and, in 1720, one on Prince Edward Island. An austere man who fasted rigorously and lived simply, Saint-Vallier was often hard on others. But nobody could fault his dedication, and at his death in 1727 the Diocese of Quebec had progressed far from the days of its infancy.

9

A Church of Mystics and Missionaries:
Marie de l'Incarnation and
Joseph Denys

NOT ONLY WAS Laval himself extraordinary; so were others who peopled the church of New France in his time. One of these was the young religious, Catherine de Saint-Augustin, declared Blessed in 1989. A child prodigy, Catherine Simon de Longpré had entered the Hospitallers of the Augustinian order at the age of 12. In 1648, when she was still just 16, she set out as a missionary for Canada, and began to nurse at the hospital in Quebec that the order had begun in 1639. Conditions were primitive, and the Iroquois attack was at its peak. Catherine's own health was fragile, but she refused to turn back. There, good-humoured and beloved, she served the sick until her early death in 1668.

But her outwardly ordinary life hid an extraordinary mysticism. Internally Catherine had lived a deep spiritual struggle in which God had permitted her to be tormented constantly by the forces of evil. She felt called to endure her sufferings for Canada and for its sins; for this she is often considered the "co-foundress" of the Canadian church. Bishop Laval himself does not let us forget Catherine the missionary: "I have no need of the extraordinary things ..." he wrote, "to be convinced of her saintliness; her real virtues make it perfectly known to me."

Extraordinary too was another contemporary of Catherine and Laval, Marie (Guyart) de l'Incarnation, beatified in 1980. Marie had married, but at 19 was left a widow with no money and an infant son. Soon she was manager of a transport business, but the call to religious life was so strong that in 1631 she put her son with her sister and joined the Ursulines. She felt that God had called her to Canada. With the assistance of a laywoman, Marie-Madeline de la Peltrie, who accompanied them and remained with them, Marie brought

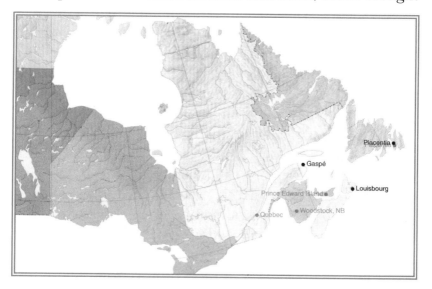

a group of her sisters to Canada in 1639. She completely devoted herself to their mission, the education of girls, French and Native. A remarkable woman, she was equally comfortable as confidante of French officials and friend of young Native women, some of whom eventually became religious sisters. Her letters (perhaps 13,000 during her life) provide a unique outlook on New France.

Even more remarkable are her mystical writings, which give a glimpse into an interior life of prayer and praise. She was endowed, in Laval's words, "with so perfect a union with God, that she preserved His presence amongst the various occupations in which her vocation involved her." She died in 1672, after saying goodbye to a group of Native girls; people of her own day considered her a saint.

Such witness began to inspire Canadian-born women to enter religious life. The first of these was Marie-Françoise Giffard (Marie de Saint-Ignace), who became a Hospitaller in Quebec in 1646, at the age of 12. Through much of her life as a nun she was ill, and was only 23 when she died. But she was the first of many, already 50 by 1688.

The same was true for the clergy. Joseph Denys was the first Canadian-born Récollect. Born at Trois-Rivières in 1657, Denys went to the minor seminary in Quebec, became a Récollect in 1677, then finished his studies in France. From 1683 Denys held a series of appointments that virtually spanned the entire diocese. First, he spent six years at Percé (Gaspé). From 1689 he was parish priest and vicar-general at Placentia, Newfoundland. In

1692, he founded the Récollect convent in Montreal. In 1696 he became Récollect superior in Quebec, then for five years provincial commissioner for the Récollects in Canada. From 1709 to 1717, Denys served as parish priest in Trois-Rivières. From 1727 to 1729 he resided at Louisbourg as vicar-general for Ile-Royale (Cape Breton). He died at Quebec in 1736.

From 1718, Father Denys concerned himself with the cause of Brother Didace (Claude Pelletier), a remarkable lay brother who had accompanied him in Gaspé, Placentia, and Montreal. Born at Sainte-Anne de Beaupré in 1657, and trained as a carpenter, he entered the Récollects in 1678. A notable builder, Brother Didace constructed many of the Récollect establishments. But he was even more revered for his deep and simple piety, and from his death in 1699 at Trois-Rivières, numerous miracles were attributed to him. In both senses he symbolized the builders of the church in New France.

10

At the Side of a People in Need: Marguerite d'Youville and Bishop Pontbriand

DURING THE 1700S Canada faced a host of problems. Some were social: alcoholism, dealings with the Natives, care of the poor and sick, education. Others were the effects of war: hardship, instability and, ultimately, the relations of the conquered to the victors.

Canadians were increasingly autonomous, and it was often local people of faith who addressed these needs. Renowned among them was Marguerite (Dufrost) d'Youville. Born in 1701 at Varennes, Quebec, she later moved to Montreal and married François d'Youville, who died in 1730. To support herself and two small children Marguerite ran a trading company. Out of a deepening concern for the poor, on December 31, 1737 she and three companions pledged their lives to their service; though laypersons, they took the traditional vows.

Marguerite, who was working from her Montreal home, had to face countless difficulties, including the mocking name *"les grises"* or "tipsy women" from those who supposed their support came from the liquor trade of her in-laws. (Eventually their community, formally recognized in 1755, became *"Les Soeurs Grises"* or "Grey Nuns.") In 1747, against strong opposition, the women were given charge of the Hôpital-Général (until then for men). They rapidly reformed it, paid off its debts, and made a place of care for the sick and poor of both sexes, including "fallen women." A smallpox epidemic in 1755 made the institution a true hospital; war imposed the care of sick soldiers and British prisoners. To achieve all this, Marguerite's abilities were critical, especially when fire destroyed the building in 1765. "So much at one time:" she wrote, "to lose one's king, one's country, one's possessions." But she rebuilt, and by her death in 1771, the hospital was flourishing. In 1990, the Church acknowledged Marguerite's faith and works by declaring her a saint.

Marguerite had referred to the British conquest. In 1755 Britain and France began a war for North America that caused terrible hardship. The first to suffer were the Nova Scotia Acadians. For the most part neutral, they had lived uneasily under British rule since 1714. In 1755 Lieutenant-Governor Lawrence imposed a loyalty oath obliging them to bear arms for Britain; when they refused it, he ordered their mass deportation. About 7000 Acadians were exiled that year alone. Another 2000 to 3000 left later, including 700 from Prince Edward Island in 1758, most of whom drowned at sea. Among the deported were at least five of their priests.

Despite the deportation, some priests managed to stay with the Acadian remnant. When the British captured Fort Beauséjour, New Brunswick, in 1755, Father Jean Manach, a priest of the Missions-Étrangères, fled to the Miramachi region, where he ministered to the Acadian and Mi'kmaq fugitives. His confrere, Pierre Maillard, served on Cape Breton until the fall of Louisbourg in 1758, when he too fled to the Miramachi. A Jesuit, Father Charles Germain, was able to remain in Aukpaque on the St. John River. After 1759, feeling that the French government had abandoned Acadia, all three priests accepted peace terms from the British. While this spared their people further suffering, it brought down on them the anger of French officialdom.

With the British conquest of Canada in 1759-60, Bishop Henri-Marie Dubreil de Pontbriand likewise faced hard choices. For the welfare of the people, should he cooperate with the Protestant British rulers, or should he uphold loyalty to the French Catholic regime that had appointed him? The Acadian deportations fresh in his memory, Pontbriand decided that the church must accept the new British rule. Even before Quebec had fallen, he issued such instructions to his clergy, imposing a conciliatory policy that undoubtedly served the interests of both the church and the conquered people.

Sadly, Pontbriand died within months, leaving the church headless at a critical time. Since British law did not then tolerate Catholicism, would Britain even allow a new Catholic bishop? But London closed its eyes, and the

Quebec clergy elected as bishop Jean-Olivier Briand, the interim leader of the diocese and a candidate acceptable to the British. In 1766 Rome approved, and Briand was quietly consecrated. He continued Pontbriand's policies, producing tangible results. A government legal opinion in 1765 concluded that British laws against Catholics did not apply in Canada. In 1772 Briand was permitted to consecrate a coadjutor, Louis-Philippe Mariachau d'Esgly, the first Canadian-born bishop. Finally the Quebec Act of 1774 recognized both the "accustomed Dues and Rights" of the church and the civil rights of the Catholic people. In turn, Briand opposed the American overtures that in 1776 tried to enlist French Canada in the revolution. It was an era of painful decisions.

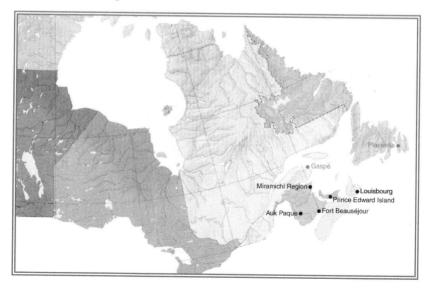

11

The Emergence of English-speaking Catholicism: James Louis O'Donel and Edmund Burke

FROM THE 1680S young Irish men and women began to migrate to Newfoundland for work in the fishery. By 1735, the governor declared "Irish Papists" the largest group in the colony. But although they numbered several thousand, they totally lacked clergy. Ecclesiastically, Newfoundland had been separated in 1713 from the Quebec diocese. It then came under English jurisdiction, but persecuted English Catholics could offer little help. Only in 1755 was Bishop Challoner in London able to send a priest, an unnamed Irish Augustinian, to Newfoundland. However, the governor immediately ordered his arrest, and although he eluded capture, buildings where Mass was celebrated were burned to the ground, and Catholics known to have attended were subjected to harsh fines and even exile.

By the late 1770s, however, the climate had changed, and several itinerant Irish priests had come to Newfoundland. In 1783, the governor approved the building of a chapel in St. John's, and the Catholics there petitioned for regular clergy. The matter went to Rome, which in May, 1784, constituted Newfoundland as a separate ecclesiastical territory (as it did the new United States a week later). Rome appointed James Louis O'Donel, an Irish Franciscan who had studied in Rome and taught in Prague, Newfoundland's first prefect-apostolic.

Newfoundland Catholics still faced official discrimination; they did not receive full civil rights until 1832. Indeed, in 1786, O'Donel himself was even wounded by an iron file thrown at him by Prince William Henry (later King William IV). Despite the difficulties, however, O'Donel was able to establish parishes, provide clergy, and put the Church on a sound footing. By 1794, the Newfoundland Church was large and stable enough that its members petitioned the Pope to have O'Donel named bishop. The next year, the Pope accepted their request, and Newfoundland became a vicariate-apostolic. On September 21, 1796, O'Donel was consecrated bishop in Quebec, becoming Canada's first English-speaking bishop, and the first bishop outside the Quebec diocese. It was a time of revolutions—France in 1789, Ireland in 1798—but O'Donel abhorred their violence, and when the Irish garrison in St. John's revolted in 1800, the bishop successfully insulated the civilian population. He resigned in 1807, but his leadership had ensured the church's growth where, not long before, Catholics had been persecuted.

After the foundation of Halifax in 1749, Irish Catholics began to immigrate to Nova Scotia as well. Likewise came the Highland Scots from the 1770s; the Catholics eventually concentrated in Antigonish County and on Cape Breton. At the same time they settled on Prince Edward Island. Although they too were under severe civil disabilities until two years later, Halifax Catholics petitioned Quebec for a priest of their own in 1782. In 1785 Bishop d'Esgly was able to appoint there Father James Jones, an Irish Capuchin; in 1787, Jones was given extensive authority over Nova Scotia, Cape Breton, Prince Edward Island and the Magdalene Islands, a recognition of the

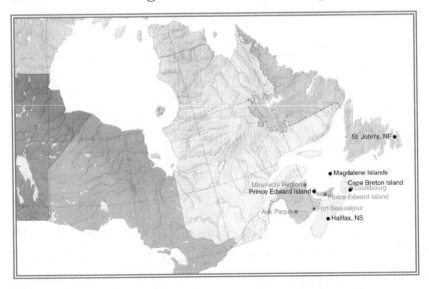

English-speaking population. Jones secured other priests to assist him, and generally brought order to church affairs in Nova Scotia until his retirement in 1800.

A year later Jones was followed by Edmund Burke, an Irish priest who had served in Quebec, and in the Detroit and Niagara areas. Burke saw the population of Nova Scotia Catholics grow to about 8,500 by 1815, about double what it had been when he had arrived. Another 7,000 were on Cape Breton, which was then a separate colony. Burke also engaged in a pamphlet war of words with Anglican and Protestant opponents. Though polemical on both sides, it gained for the church a certain intellectual respectability.

In 1815 Burke was asked to report to Rome on the state of the church in the Maritimes. He emphasized the shortage of priests and the difficulties of recruitment. With the agreement of the Bishop of Quebec, Rome accepted his suggestion that Nova Scotia become a separate jurisdiction, and in 1817 Burke was appointed its first bishop and vicar-apostolic. Burke himself died in 1820. No successor was named until 1827, when the Scottish priest William Fraser was appointed. Bishop Fraser decided to remain in Antigonish, where he felt the Scots community needed him. The Irish in Halifax resented this, and after bitter divisions, the diocese, which by then included Cape Breton and Bermuda, was separated into two in 1845: Halifax and Arichat (later Antigonish). The circumstances were regrettable, but the move recognized two ethnic Catholic groups that by then had become significant.

12

Joseph-Octave Plessis and the Reorganization of the Canadian Church

THE SITUATIONS of Newfoundland and Nova Scotia indicated the need for new models of church organization. No one understood this more than the Bishop of Quebec, Joseph-Octave Plessis, who presided over a diocese both too large and too diverse to ensure proper pastoral care. It also faced a chronic shortage of priests: Canadian vocations were low, and the government restricted the entry of foreigners. Plessis had consented to the separation of Nova Scotia, but he had a larger vision. At the time, both London and Rome had agreed to vicariates for Upper Canada and Prince Edward Island, but Plessis felt that further isolated vicariates would weaken the church. His thought was that Quebec should become an archdiocese with proper suffragan dioceses, including additional sees at Montreal and Red River. The bishop attempted to negotiate this with London, but in 1819 Rome unilaterally named him Archbishop, which offended the British. The most he could obtain was a compromise: bishops in each of the four areas, but no new dioceses.

Thus arose the unusual situation in which four new bishops governed large parts of Canada, although technically they were only vicars-general because the dioceses had not been formed. Thus in 1820 Alexander Macdonell became bishop for Upper Canada, Jean-Jacques Lartigue bishop in Montreal, Angus Bernard MacEachern bishop for Prince Edward Island and much of the Maritimes; Joseph-Norbert Provencher became the first bishop in the vast Canadian west. These makeshift arrangements largely succeeded, although the Quebec's authority and responsibility remained an uncertain factor.

Such provisions were urgently needed in Upper Canada, where there were some 20,000 Catholic people. Macdonell had gone there in 1804 with settlers from a Highland regiment to which he had been chaplain. A staunch British supporter, his salary came from the government, and his relations with the authorities were excellent. Macdonell had been vicar-general for Upper Canada, and knew the territory well. Good connections enabled him to acquire excellent church sites in such developing towns as Kingston, York (Toronto) and Guelph.

As bishop, Macdonell especially devoted himself to securing support for priests and teachers. He readily obtained Irish priests for the Irish communities in York and the Ottawa Valley, but he was sometimes at odds with the Irish elements, largely because their politics were more radical than his own. In reward for Macdonell's loyalty, London soon withdrew its previous objections to a new diocese, and in 1826 the Holy See established the diocese of Kingston, the first in British territory since the Reformation. Similarly, in 1830, the government named the bishop to the Upper Canada Legislative Council. Although in the late 1830s Macdonell used his influence to dissuade Catholics from supporting the radical party, he was critical of political greed. He put the church in Ontario on a firm foundation, and a year after his death in 1840, the diocese was judged large and secure enough to be subdivided, with central and western Ontario becoming the new diocese of Toronto.

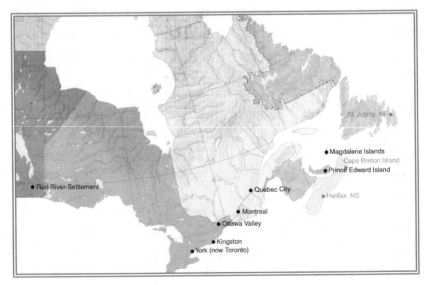

The new bishop for Prince Edward Island faced a far different situation. MacEachern came from a Highland family that had moved to the Island in 1772. He stayed in Scotland to study secretly for the priesthood, but rejoined his family in 1790. The colony had been without a priest for five years, and MacEachern served not only the Island itself, but also Highland communities in Cape Breton and parts of Nova Scotia. He occasionally had help, but even in 1808 he was the only priest in the colony.

As bishop from 1821, MacEachern supervised not only Prince Edward Island, but also New Brunswick and the Magdalene Islands. Speaking Gaelic, English and French, and willing to travel, his talents were suited to the task. His preoccupation was to provide clergy, especially local vocations, but he had limited success. He was largely dependent on immigrant Irish priests (who were British subjects), but their quality varied. MacEachern fought consistently for an independent diocese, which he achieved in 1829, when Rome made the whole territory the Diocese of Charlottetown. This did not resolve the difficulty of providing for the Acadians and Irish of New Brunswick, but Fredericton would become a separate diocese in 1842. Always a missionary and a man of the people, MacEachern died in 1835. His tenure as a bishop vividly illustrated the difficulties of a poor and far-flung diocese. Though not in the orderly way he intended, Plessis' vision was being realized.

13

Provencher at the Red River

THE MOST imaginative part of Plessis' strategy was the naming of a bishop for the Canadian northwest. Indeed, there were only two priests in the territory, which, moreover, was in a state of armed conflict. Much of the area formed "Rupert's Land," granted to the Hudson's Bay Company in 1670. Although the company had numerous trading posts, it did not encourage European settlement until 1812, when it sponsored a Scots colony at Point Douglas (Winnipeg). This angered the rival North West Company, who feared settlement would interfere with the fur trade. Sharp clashes ensued, including a massacre of settlers in 1816.

In 1818 Plessis sent to the northwest Joseph-Norbert Provencher, a native of Nicolet. Provencher made his headquarters on the Red River, at the junction of the Assiniboine, where he constructed a chapel dedicated to Boniface, who had christianized the German tribes. His initial efforts were well received. Plessis recalled him to Quebec in 1820, and informed the 33-year-old priest that he had been named bishop. Provencher, however, took months before accepting, feeling the call "obviously beyond my strength and my ability." He was eventually consecrated at Trois-Rivières in 1822.

When he returned to St. Boniface, Provencher faced a far better situation than he had left: the fighting between the rival companies had ended with their merger. His priorities could now become evangelization and education. His people were diverse—whites, Métis, and Natives—and although he did not speak the Native languages, Provencher endeavoured to reach out to all. Evangelization advanced slowly, for it faced many difficulties, including general acceptance among the Métis of common-law unions, but there was gradual progress. By the 1830s the church in the northwest, though small in numbers, was well established.

Provencher was committed to educating both girls and boys, and to providing useful instruction in the trades. Father Jean Harper initially taught both genders, but in 1829, Provencher opened the St. Boniface School for girls, directed by Angélique and Marguerite Nolin, two Métis women. The "Misses Nolin," who had some schooling in Montreal, spoke French, English, Ojibwa and Cree. For the next twenty years they taught a group of largely Métis and Native children, as well as assisting missionary Father George-Antoine Bellcourt both to learn the native languages and to prepare an Ojibwa dictionary and texts. Provencher's interest in the education of women also led him to bring to Red River in 1844 a group of Grey Nuns under Mother Marie-Louise Valade. She was a wonderfully practical woman whose sisters not only educated the community, but also served the needs of the poor, the aged and the sick.

By 1837 Provencher's concern also embraced the Columbia country to the west of the Rockies. Technically it was not within his jurisdiction, but the settlers there had asked for clergy. He was instrumental in the mission to the west coast the next year of Fathers Modeste Demers and François-Norbert Blanchet. But adequate clergy were always lacking. Provencher tried, without success in his lifetime, to foster local vocations. His priests were largely diocesan clergy from Quebec who often went as they came. By 1843 he still had only four, one of whom was murdered by Natives the next year. The instability of an itinerant secular clergy led him in 1844 to approach the saintly

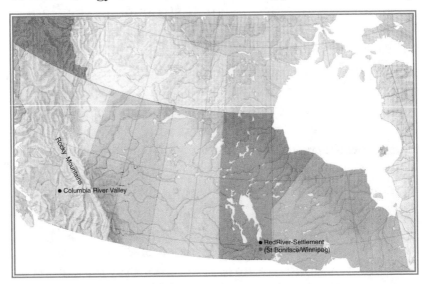

Eugène de Mazenod, bishop of Marseilles and founder of the Oblates of Mary Immaculate. The following year, two Oblates, Pierre Aubert and the Canadian-born Alexandre-Antonin Taché, reached Red River, and three more followed shortly. This beginning was to have tremendous impact on future missionary efforts in the Canadian northwest.

Perhaps fearing autonomy would curtail his supply of priests from the east, Provencher did not rush to regularize the ecclesiastical status of the northwest, which was still part of the Quebec diocese. However in 1843 he and Archbishop Signay agreed that the time had come to make the territory a vicariate-apostolic, which was done the next year. In 1846 Rome constituted the whole of the west coast as the ecclesiastical province of Oregon, under Archbishop Blanchet; it was made up of three dioceses with a total Catholic population of just 6000. Provencher resisted a proposal that the same should happen in his territory. Nevertheless, in 1847 the vicariate became the Diocese of the Northwest. In 1851 it was renamed the Diocese of St. Boniface, a testimony to both its simple beginnings and the efforts of its founder.

14

Reshaping the Church in Quebec: Ignace Bourget

THE LAST ELEMENT of Plessis' design was a diocese for Montreal. Lartigue, the bishop there, was quick to show his independence, and fought hard for the separate diocese that Plessis intended. Taking a harder attitude than the archbishop, Lartigue maintained that British consent should be ignored, and that the church should just confront government with a *fait accompli*. His position was vindicated when in 1836 Rome unilaterally established the diocese of Montreal; London had no choice but to accept the reality.

Ignace Bourget (1779-1885), coadjutor from 1837 and Lartigue's successor in 1840, was also his disciple. As a promoter of the church's autonomy, Bourget shared both his predecessor's disregard for British wishes and his hostility to the liberal *patriote* ideology. In many ways, Bourget, like Bishop Michael Anthony Fleming in Newfoundland, brought to the church in Canada a new face. These men now proposed to end the church's subservient status. "In the 70 years of conquest, religion in this country has almost always lost the advantage through fright," Bourget wrote in 1830.

An autonomous church and a diocese of almost 190,000 Catholics required strong institutions, which in Bourget's view were greatly lacking. He appealed to the newly-vibrant religious congregations of France: he brought back the Jesuits to Canada, and he introduced the Oblates and the Sisters of the Sacred Heart. At home, Bourget supported the foundation of the Sisters of Providence, Sisters of the Holy Names of Jesus and Mary, Sisters of Mercy, and Sisters of St. Ann. He established the periodical *Mélanges Religieux* to propound the church's views. The resulting clerical and religious presence in educational and other institutions gave the church a powerful influence.

To unite the dioceses of Canada, Bourget also promoted the establishment of an ecclesiastical province. This was done in 1844, with an archdiocese at Quebec, and Kingston, Montreal, Toronto, and New Brunswick as suffragans. The Northwest was added in 1847; the new diocese of Bytown (Ottawa) under the Oblate bishop, Joseph-Bruno Guigues, in 1848. Finally in 1852 came the dioceses of Trois-Rivières and Saint-Hyacinthe.

Bourget's conservative or "ultramontane" convictions deepened after 1849, when revolution struck the Papal States. He staunchly supported the Pope's temporal power, and vigorously attacked the liberal views at home that used the occasion not only to advocate separation of church and state, but also to oppose clerical control in the social and political orders. He replaced customary French usages with Roman devotions and liturgical practices. Montreal's magnificent St. James Cathedral (later Mary Queen of the World), built to replace the church burnt in 1852, was thus modeled after St. Peter's Basilica. In 1868 Bourget championed Bishop Guigues' plan to raise an army of Papal Zouaves who went from Quebec to defend the Papal States.

Conflicts were frequent. Bourget alienated influential laity who resented what they considered clerical interference in politics. He fought with the Sulpicians over their traditional privileges, and deposed Blessed Esther Blondin, foundress of the Sisters of St. Ann. He battled Laval University over its failure to establish a Montreal branch under his control. His relationships with the archbishops of Quebec were also poor: Bourget bluntly had told Signay to resign; Taschereau, a past rector of Laval, thought Bourget's opinions extreme.

Bourget's influence was widespread. One prominent supporter was Bishop Louis-François Laflèche of Trois-Rivières. Laflèche had served twelve years in the Northwest, then as seminary professor in Nicolet and as vicar-general. In 1866 he became coadjutor, and in 1870 diocesan bishop. Participating in Vatican I, he declared its acceptance of papal infallibility "the finest day" of his life. Like Bourget, Laflèche was suspicious of the "liberalism" of Laval University, and he resisted the separation of the new diocese of Nicolet from Trois-Rivières. (It occurred, over his objections, in 1885). These positions led to open conflict with Archbishop Taschereau. Laflèche promoted French Canadian nationalism and a Catholic culture; he spoke passionately on public issues, including Confederation, which he supported. His ministry in the Northwest made him especially vocal on the Manitoba schools question; so much so that in 1896 he condemned the Liberal politician Wilfrid Laurier as at odds with Catholic teaching.

Both Bourget and Laflèche were energetic and truly dedicated bishops who recognized the new strength of the Church in Quebec. They sought to harness that strength to build there a Christian civilization on Catholic principles. Their views, representing one side of a struggle for the soul of Quebec Catholicism, had tremendous influence; in the end, however, more moderate positions usually prevailed.

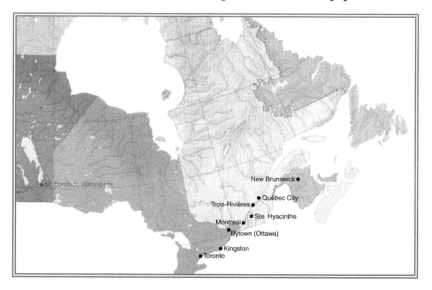

15

The Church in the Northwest:
Alexandre-Antonin Taché and Louis Riel

PROVENCHER'S FIRST choice as his successor had been Laflèche, whose illness prompted him to decline. Provencher turned instead to the 27-year-old Oblate, Alexandre-Antonin Taché, who in 1850 was named coadjutor. In 1853, when Provencher died, Taché took charge of the diocese. He was then at Île-à-la-Crosse, Saskatchewan, supervising the mission, and did not return to St. Boniface for another year.

Hoping to evangelize the Native peoples, and seeking to counteract the already active Protestant missionaries, Taché promoted a strong western outreach. By 1856 there were missions at Lac Ste. Anne, Lac La Biche and Fort Chipewyan (Alberta), Fort Resolution (N.W.T.), and Île-à-la-Crosse. To oversee that area, Taché sought a coadjutor; for this Vital Grandin, a 28-year-old Oblate, was named bishop in 1857. By 1860, St. Albert, near Fort Edmonton, had become the western missionary centre. In 1862, at the initiative of Taché and Grandin, the district of Athabaska-Mackenzie (Grouard-McLellan) became a separate vicariate, with Henri Faraud, another Oblate, as its bishop.

The Northwest missions depended upon energetic and often heroic Oblates, who by 1861 numbered 30. They included the young Father Pierre-Henri Grollier, who died in 1864, aged just 38, after a twelve-year missionary career that took him throughout Alberta and Saskatchewan, and then into the Northwest Territories, where he founded several missions, including Fort Good Hope beyond the Arctic Circle. On the other hand, Father Albert Lacombe, whose ministry in the west had begun at age 22 in 1849, eventually celebrated his priestly diamond jubilee. He was wounded in a battle between the Blackfoot and the Cree in 1865, helped bring the railway across the prairies, became a pastor in Calgary and Edmonton, and in 1900 negotiated with the Austrian Emperor Franz-Joseph for Ukrainian clergy.

The Grey Nuns were no less daring. By 1850 they had expanded beyond St. Boniface itself. They soon established schools and orphanages for Native children at more remote sites like St. Albert, Providence on the Mackenzie River, and Fort Resolution on Great Slave Lake.

In 1869, as Canada negotiated with the Hudson's Bay Company and Britain to annex the Northwest, Taché feared for the Métis. He worried that without safeguards, Anglo-Protestants, many of whom despised the Métis, would soon predominate. Ottawa ignored his proposals. While Taché was in Rome for the Vatican Council, rebellion broke out, and Louis Riel organized a provisional government. Until 1865 Riel had studied for the priesthood; young, educated, bilingual and religious, he rapidly

became the Métis leader. To mediate, the federal government called Taché from Rome and made him its delegate;
he was to restore calm, ease the transfer of the Northwest
to Canada, and proclaim an amnesty.

During this process, three delegates, led by the gifted
Father Noël-Joseph Ritchot, negotiated the admission of
Manitoba into Confederation. They secured reasonable
terms, which Riel and the provisional government
accepted. Amnesty, however, became a burning issue.
Taché maintained that Ottawa had guaranteed a general
amnesty, but this was never written. The provisional government had executed Thomas Scott, an Ulster Orange-
man, and Anglo-Protestant Ontario would not accept
amnesty for those responsible. Riel, Ritchot, and Taché
felt betrayed, and Riel sought safety in the United States.

Twice elected to Parliament, although never taking his
seat, Riel lived a harried existence. He became increasingly
overtaken by a messianic complex, and spent time in an
asylum. In 1884 the Métis invited him to return to the
South Saskatchewan, where land disputes had produced
major grievances against the federal government. The
clergy, including Grandin and Taché, supported the Métis,
but not violence. In 1885 Riel publicly broke with the
church and proclaimed his visionary theology. Violence
soon erupted; some Cree joined the Métis, until Canadian
militia crushed the rebellion at Batoche. Riel was captured
and was hanged in Regina after a trial that Wilfrid Laurier

called "judicial murder." Attended in prison by Father Lacombe, he died reconciled with the church.

The Northwest events led to vicious anti-French and anti-Catholic reaction in Ontario, and a sense of outrage in Quebec. In Manitoba, anti-Catholicism paved the way in 1890 for the Greenway government to abolish Catholic public schools. Taché fought this determinedly both politically and in the courts, for he felt the law violated the principles under which Manitoba had entered Confederation. He was still fighting this battle when he died in 1894. Today his remains and Riel's lie near each other in St. Boniface, joining in death two figures whose lives were devoted, in different ways, to the cause of justice.

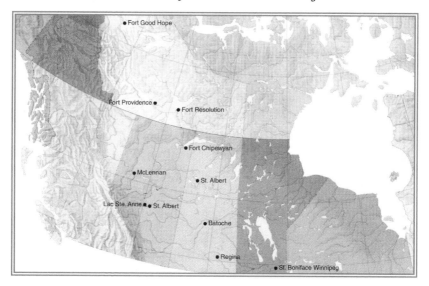

16

Defending the Faith:
John Joseph Lynch in Toronto

"AS LONG AS THE Catholic Religion and its children appear to be in a condition of poverty, we will make but slow progress," wrote Michael Power, Toronto's first bishop, in 1846. Toronto had only one parish, and Power had recently begun St. Michael's Cathedral. He never saw it finished, for he died the next year from typhus brought by Irish immigrants fleeing the potato famine.

In a society where other Christian denominations were firmly established, strong Catholic institutions became important. Both Power and his successor, the French-born Armand-François-Marie de Charbonnel, recognized this completely. To this end, they introduced into Toronto religious congregations, including the Jesuits, the Basilians, Loretto Sisters, Sisters of St. Joseph, and Christian Brothers. Charbonnel successfully championed a separate Catholic school system for Upper Canada; he also laid the basis for many of Ontario's future Catholic institutions.

The religious often encountered real hardships. Five Irish Sisters of Loretto, for example, arrived in the midst of the typhus epidemic. Two weeks later, Bishop Power, who had sponsored them, was dead, and the diocese could not support them. They had to organize a private school for girls, from which they supported a free school. By 1851, three of the five had died. But one, Mother Teresa Dease, lived until 1889; by then there were 13 Loretto foundations in Ontario. The Sisters of St. Joseph, who came from Philadelphia in 1851, survived and flourished despite similar difficulties; they lost their own superior, Mother Delphine Fontbonne, to typhus in 1856. By 1862, however, they were well established in both the Toronto and Hamilton dioceses, with numerous vocations.

Geography and population growth prompted Charbonnel to request two new dioceses in Ontario. This step was taken in 1856, with Bishop John Farrell being named to Hamilton, and Pierre-Adolphe Pinsoneault to London (Ontario). Bishop Pinsoneault was a controversial figure. He loathed Charbonnel, and frequently quarreled with his own clergy and religious. In 1859 he had the diocese transferred to Sandwich (Windsor, Ontario, today). Pinsoneault was obliged to resign in 1866; the see returned to London in 1869.

In 1860 Charbonnel had resigned, uneasy about serving a largely Irish population. His successor was his Irish-born coadjutor, John Joseph Lynch, appointed a year earlier. Lynch led the church through a turbulent period; anti-Catholicism was then rampant throughout Canada, especially where Catholics were a minority. George Brown, editor of the Toronto *Globe*, had already spearheaded a "No Popery" campaign in 1850, and these attitudes persisted. In 1865, Lynch described Toronto Catholicism as "in combat with bigotry, pride, poverty and orang[e]ism."

Bigotry intensified after 1869-70, as a result of two separate events: the declaration of papal infallibility in Rome, and the execution of Thomas Scott in Manitoba. The Toronto Orange Lodge described Scott as "murdered by the enemies of our Queen, country and religion," and wanted government to save the Northwest "from those who have turned it over to Popery." In the 1880s, both the nationalism of Premier Mercier in Quebec and the Northwest rebellion provoked similar outbursts. Lynch challenged such anti-Catholicism through a series of Sunday

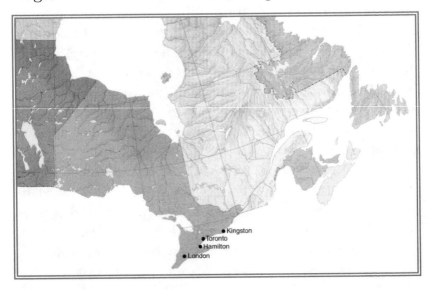

lectures that drew large crowds and made him an un-questioned champion of Catholic rights.

Ontario Catholics were increasing. In 1870, Toronto received metropolitan status, with Kingston, Hamilton and London as suffragan dioceses. In 1874, Archbishop Lynch and Bishop Guigues of Ottawa persuaded Rome to create the vicariate of Northern Canada (eventually the Peterborough diocese). In 1886, Ottawa became an archdiocese and, in 1889, Kingston became a separate ecclesiastical province. Alexandria and the apostolic vicariate of Pontiac (later Pembroke) date from 1890.

Lynch died in 1888; his successor was Archbishop John Walsh. Although they faced similar problems, Walsh addressed them differently. As bishop of London, he had restored tranquility. At the same time, though unable to attend Vatican I, Walsh eloquently defended papal infallibility. In Toronto he found anti-Catholicism much alive; at his installation young Orangemen threw stones at his carriage. Walsh's policy was to avoid confrontation when the inevitable outcome would just place the Catholic minority in a worse position. Appalled by the abolition of funding for Manitoba's Catholic schools, Walsh feared similar Protestant agitation in Ontario. He thus limited his public protests, and rode out the controversy. At his death in 1898 the condition of the Ontario church had advanced immeasurably from Power's time. Laity, religious and priests had worked hard to achieve this; they did not lack energetic episcopal leadership.

17

Confederation and the Council: Thomas Connolly and the Church in the Maritimes

THE YOUNG IRISH Capuchin Thomas Louis Connolly had come to Halifax in 1842 with William Walsh, the coadjutor bishop. His talents were soon recognized, and in 1852 he succeeded William Dollard, first bishop of Fredericton. That diocese had been established ten years earlier, when Charlottetown was divided, and Bishop Bernard Donald MacDonald chose to stay there. Connolly resided in Saint John, where Dollard had moved to care for the large Irish influx following the potato famine, but the diocese included the whole province, with its mixed French, Irish and Native Catholic population. The Maritimes had just become Canada's second ecclesiastical province, under Halifax, with Charlottetown, Arichat and Saint John as suffragans.

Connolly was not long in Saint John; Archbishop Walsh died in 1858, and his former protégé became his successor in Halifax. The diocese of Chatham (later Bathurst), under Bishop James Rogers, was soon added to his suffragan sees; the division of New Brunswick into two dioceses was a first step toward recognizing its distinct language groups.

The new archbishop had worked hard for Catholic education in Saint John, and continued his efforts in Halifax. The Religious of the Sacred Heart and the Sisters of Charity were already active in the diocese, and to complement them, he introduced the Christian Brothers. He also waged an ongoing battle for publicly funded Catholic separate schools. A compromise eventually produced *de facto* Catholic schools within the public system, but without the legal protection Connolly wanted. Here Connolly faced strong anti-Catholic opposition, but his policy was to speak consistently for tolerance. Because of its violence, he even denounced the Fenian movement, despite its Irish Catholic roots.

Connolly passionately encouraged Confederation. He spoke of Canadians having an identity, "a name to go abroad with." He believed that shared resources would benefit the poor. And he felt that the interests of Catholics, a minority everywhere outside Quebec, would be better protected. Canada's other bishops also generally supported Confederation, but without Connolly's enthusiasm. In Newfoundland, John Thomas Mullock and John Dalton were probably opposed. Bishops Rogers and Sweeney in New Brunswick had to be persuaded; the Quebec bishops also persuaded them that education should be a provincial matter. In 1866-67 Connolly went to London to promote Confederation and to ensure that the arrangements protected Catholic schools. He was both influential and remarkably successful, obtaining important concessions for Ontario, although, ironically, not for Catholic schools in Nova Scotia.

He was equally vocal against the movement for repeal of Confederation in Nova Scotia, although only unyielding British policy defeated it. Although Nova Scotia stayed in, Newfoundland voted against Confederation in 1869. Prince Edward Island had opted out also, but in 1873 financial difficulties obliged it to enter the union. Another strong Confederate, Bishop Peter McIntyre, had rallied Catholic support, but he also failed in his efforts to have publicly supported Catholic schools made part of the terms. The New Brunswick bishops had experienced a similar setback in 1871.

In 1869-70 Connolly was one of 16 Canadian bishops to attend the First Vatican Council. Along with Rogers and Sweeney, he opposed the definition of papal infallibility as both unnecessary and lacking any basis in Church tradition. Rather than vote against it, Connolly left the Council; afterwards, however, he felt morally bound to support the doctrine. He died in 1876, at only 61; a Presbyterian minister said simply: "Canada [has] lost a patriot."

Not only papal authority, but also that of the bishops was sometimes an issue. Bishop Enrico Carfagnini of Harbour Grace, Newfoundland, an Italian named during the Vatican Council, provoked enormous opposition when he tried to take control of the local Irish society. Rome ruled against him in 1875, and in 1879 forced him to resign. Similarly, Connolly's successor in Halifax, Michael Hannan, became embroiled in an unseemly battle with the Sisters of Charity, whom he disliked: he attempted to interfere in what they considered internal affairs. Extreme positions were taken: in one parish the sisters were not allowed in church, and parents were told to boycott their school. However, the archbishop met his match in Mother Mary Francis Maguire, their superior. She appealed to the Holy See, which named Bishop John Cameron of Arichat to investigate. Cameron's report was highly critical of Hannan, and in 1880 Rome sided with the sisters. Whether political or religious, controversies were a mark of the times.

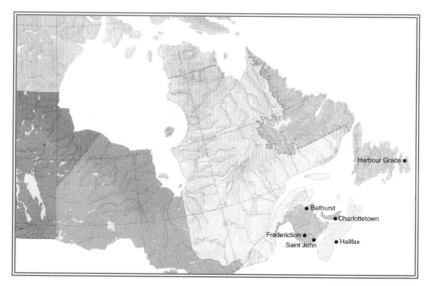

18

A Church from Sea to Sea: Demers and Durieu on the Pacific Coast

BRITISH COLUMBIA'S first resident priests were Spanish missionaries at the San Lorenzo de Nutka outpost on Vancouver Island, but this lasted only from 1789 to 1795. Canadian settlement began soon after, at trading posts of the North West Company and its successor, the Hudson's Bay Company. Although many of the original settlers were French Canadian and Métis Catholics, clergy did not follow them.

In 1837, however, Archbishop Signay of Quebec appointed Father François-Norbert Blanchet as vicar-general for the "Oregon territory," the vast Canadian and U.S. Pacific northwest. The next year Blanchet journeyed overland to the Pacific with Father Modeste Demers, who had been at Red River. Demers learned Native languages easily, and for several years he ventured into the British Columbia interior, making converts among the aboriginal people. In 1844 the mission received help from the Jesuit,

Pierre-Jean De Smet, who, having visited the year before, brought additional priests and sisters from his native Belgium. Among them was Father John Nobili, S.J., who until 1848 served in the interior, venturing north to Babine Lake, and baptizing over 1,300 Natives of various nations.

In 1843 the Oregon territory became a vicariate, with Blanchet as bishop, and in 1846 he had it made an ecclesiastical province. Demers thought this premature, for it effectively made the area dependent on its own resources, but he accepted to become bishop of Vancouver (Island) and administrator for the mainland. Initially Demers lacked even minimal human and financial resources, but in 1858 he was able to persuade the Oblates to establish themselves at Esquimalt, and the Sisters of St. Ann to come to Victoria.

The two congregations brought new life to the diocese. The Oblates, under Father Louis d'Herbomez, worked with Natives, with whites in now-bustling Victoria, and with gold miners in the Fraser Valley. The Oblates established Native missions at Esquimalt, New Westminster and Fort Rupert; for the whites they set up parishes and schools. The sisters, under Sister Marie du Sacré-Coeur (Salomée Valois) who served there until her death in 1906, organized a school open to girls of Native, white and mixed race origin. She also established an orphanage, and later, in 1876, a hospital; the last was noted for welcoming Chinese and Japanese patients. Her companion, Sister Marie-Angèle Gauthier, had great influence among the Coast Salish people at Duncan.

Demers died in 1871, just days after British Columbia entered Confederation. His successor, named in 1873, was Charles John Seghers, one of several Belgian priests who had responded to Demers' request for missionaries. In 1878, he became coadjutor to Archbishop Blanchet in Oregon City, but chose to return to his old diocese in 1885. Seghers vigorously promoted the Native missions, including those in Alaska and the Yukon; a crazed companion murdered him during a mission voyage to Alaska in 1886.

In 1863, the mainland had become a separate vicariate, based in New Westminster, with d'Herbomez, who was still Oblate superior, as bishop. In 1865, d'Herbomez withdrew the Oblates from Vancouver Island, a move that benefited the mainland, and by 1869 he had 55 Native

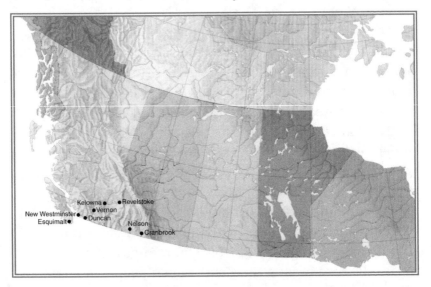

chapels. He strongly advocated reserves for the Native peoples, with industrial and agricultural boarding schools to serve them. With the building of the transcontinental railway in the 1880s, d'Herbomez addressed the additional needs of both the construction workers and the growing terminus city of Vancouver.

Until his death in 1890, d'Herbomez' Native missions had only limited success, but they laid a good foundation. His successor, Paul Durieu, another Oblate who had been his coadjutor since 1875, continued d'Herbomez' policies. The Oblates promoted temperance, stressed the use of music and Native languages, instituted Native catechists and moral watchmen. Ultimately they envisaged settled agricultural villages, although they realized this would take time. Durieu produced substantial catechetical materials, songs, prayers and biblical stories in the Native languages, and encouraged the adaptation of Native practices; notable were the huge annual retreats he arranged at mission centres.

To serve both the immigrant and Native populations, Durieu eventually had 36 Oblate priests and lay brothers, and four communities of sisters, including a novitiate for Native sisters. They served 70 Native villages, and mining towns as far flung as Cranbrook, Nelson, Revelstoke, Vernon and Kelowna. Just four years after Durieu's death in 1899, British Columbia became an ecclesiastical province, with Victoria its archbishopric. This was moved in 1908 to Vancouver; Victoria became its suffragan. In just 60 years, the local church had changed dramatically.

19

Elzéar-Alexandre Taschereau: Canada's First Cardinal

WHILE RELIGIOUS practice was strong, nineteenth century Quebec Catholicism showed serious divisions
between so-called "ultramontanes" and "liberals." These
concerned such issues as Laval University, use of funds
from the Jesuit estates, the extent to which Quebec
society should be a Catholic theocracy, clerical involvement in politics, and even the widespread French-
Canadian emigration to the United States, which some
saw as abandoning the culture in which the faith was
rooted.

Laval University, established in 1852, thought itself
the flagship of Catholic higher education in Quebec. It
sought to serve the province overall by the affiliation of
classical colleges. This was unacceptable to Bishop Bourget of Montreal, who fought tenaciously for a local
Catholic university. In 1862, and again in 1865, Rome
had to decide the issue, which it did in Laval's favour.
Laval's chief defender, one of its founders and its rector
since 1860, was Elzéar-Alexandre Taschereau. Roman-

educated and urbane, Taschereau repeatedly made the case that duplication would only ruin Laval.

In 1870, Rome chose Taschereau as Archbishop of Quebec, but he led a divided episcopate. Some bishops endorsed the "ultramontane" principle, as put by the Jesuit Édouard Hamon, that there must be "close union between the leaders of the people and the representatives of divine authority." Taschereau was more willing to suspend judgment, and he absolutely opposed clerical involvement in politics. His opponents saw the first as tolerating error, and the second as a sign of liberal leanings. In 1875 Taschereau wrote the Quebec bishops' pastoral condemning Catholic liberalism, but the next year declared unilaterally that this did not apply to the Liberal party. His suffragans, some suspicious of any liberalism, felt Taschereau had undermined them, and Bishop Laflèche even obtained a papal letter praising the original condemnation.

In 1877, to appease Liberal politicians and to resolve divisions within the church, Rome sent the Irish bishop, George Conroy, as apostolic delegate. The delegate publicly absolved the Liberal party, and inspired a directive demanding clerical prudence in political matters. This strengthened Taschereau's hand, but differences persisted. In 1883-84 another apostolic commissioner, Dom Henri Smeulders, a Belgian, tended to side with Laflèche, but Taschereau was able to use his influence in Rome to circumvent Smeulders' report. Greater unity came only after 1886, when Montreal became an ecclesiastical province, giving it more autonomy in university matters, and Pope Leo XIII made Taschereau the first Canadian cardinal.

Taschereau's strength soon began to fail (he died in 1898), and in 1891 he turned over authority to his coadjutor, Louis-Nazaire Bégin. Bégin, an energetic leader and himself a cardinal from 1914, would head the church in Canada until his death in 1925. Deeply committed to Catholic minority rights, he was soon called to defend them. In 1895, a Privy Council decision ruled that Ottawa could pass remedial legislation restoring denominational schools in Manitoba. Prime Minister Tupper, a Conservative, introduced such legislation in 1896, but Laurier's Liberals blocked its passage, and then won the next election.

The Quebec bishops had issued a pastoral obliging Catholics to vote for candidates backing remedial legislation. There was some support from the Maritimes also. Then and thereafter, however, Ontario's bishops kept a thunderous silence. Following the election, Laurier and Premier Greenway quickly agreed upon minor concessions, but did not reinstate minority rights. Archbishop Adélard Langevin of St. Boniface was outraged, and Bégin called the agreement "absolutely immoral." Pressed by Laurier, a Catholic, who spoke of clerical interference, Rome appointed a new apostolic delegate, Msgr. Rafael Merry del Val, in 1897. His report, influenced by Ontario and political in tone, became the basis of Pope Leo XIII's encyclical that urged acceptance of the Laurier-Greenway pact despite its defects.

In 1899 Diomede Falconio became the first resident apostolic delegate, but his own negotiations to improve the Laurier-Greenway agreement failed completely. Similar battles erupted in 1905 over denominational schools in the new provinces of Saskatchewan and Alberta, and in 1912, when Manitoba was extended to include the Keewatin district. In 1916, the Manitoba government abrogated even the Laurier-Greenway accord.

These matters demonstrated the need for episcopal unity throughout the country. To this end, at Rome's request, Archbishop Bégin presided over the Plenary Council of Quebec (1909) that assembled 40 Canadian bishops and diocesan administrators. However, although the Council passed 688 decrees, few of these touched the real divisions that existed; exceptions concerned bilingualism in seminaries and the care of immigrants. Unfortunately, crucial differences would persist into the future.

20

Blessed Nykyta Budka and the Struggle to Establish the Ukrainian Catholic Church

THE UKRAINIAN Catholic immigrants who began to arrive in Canada during the 1890s came without clergy. This stemmed from problems in the United States, whose bishops would not accept married Ukrainian priests. "The possible loss of a few souls of the Greek rite bears no proportion to the blessings resulting from uniformity of discipline," the American hierarchy told Rome. In 1894 the Vatican made Ukrainian clergy subject to the Latin bishops, thus provoking great resentment, and prohibited married clergy from coming to America, effectively depriving Ukrainians of their priests.

The first of several priests from the United States, Nestor Dymytriw, visited communities in Manitoba and Alberta in 1897. Two years later, Father Damascin Polivka arrived in Winnipeg to serve Ukrainian Catholics, but left after difficulties with the 15 Polish Oblates who supported Archbishop Langevin's policy of assimilation. In 1901,

Father Basil Zholdak, secretary to Metropolitan Andrei Sheptytsky, head of the Ukrainian Catholic Church, came to Canada to assess the situation. Zholdak found confusion, with many Catholics turning Orthodox, especially in Alberta. While acknowledging that Ukrainian priests who feared Latinization had sometimes caused problems, he felt that having Ukrainian clergy responsible to their own church authorities was the only solution.

Several groups proselytized among Ukrainian Catholics: atheistic *"radycaly"* urged them to leave belief in the old country; Russian Orthodox, subsidized by the Czar, promoted "pan-Slavism" and warned against vesting property with the Latins; the Independent Greek Church, founded with Presbyterian backing, tried to use Eastern practices to secretly promote Protestantism. Lacking religious leaders, many Ukrainians abandoned their Catholic roots.

In 1902, Zholdak, now apostolic visitor, returned with three Ukrainian Basilian priests (who as religious, were celibate), one lay brother, and four Sisters Servants of Mary Immaculate. These went to Alberta, where the need was greatest and Bishop Emile Legal supportive; in 1903 two more Basilians went to Winnipeg, where Langevin was now more favourable to Ukrainian clergy. In 1899 he had secured Redemptorists in Brussels to work among immigrants, including Father Achille Delaere, who served the Ukrainians around Brandon and then at Yorkton, Saskatchewan. Delaere quickly learned the language, and in 1906 was permitted to transfer to the Ukrainian rite. Three more Belgians soon joined him on the prairies, founding the Ukrainian branch of the Redemptorist order. Several French-Canadian priests similarly transferred to the Ukrainian church.

There was growing pressure for a Ukrainian bishop, as Zholdak had suggested in 1903. Fathers Dalaere and Boels, another Redemptorist, actively promoted this at the Council of Quebec in 1909, and then, following Metropolitan Sheptytsky's visit to Canada in 1910, in representations to Rome. Pressed by the apostolic delegate, Langevin eventually agreed. On July 12, 1912, Bishop Nykyta (Nicetas) Budka, 35, was named Ukrainian Catholic bishop for Canada, with Winnipeg his see. Unlike his American counterpart, he was independent of the Latin hierarchy.

Upon his arrival in Canada, Budka found twelve Ukrainian-born priests (including five Basilians), four Belgian Redemptorists, and five French Canadians serving perhaps 150,000 Ukrainian Catholics with 80 churches. The new bishop, who had previously worked with emigrants, began extensive visitations, and gradually brought order to his vast diocese.

Unfortunately, Budka's tenure was soon overshadowed by controversy. Austria-Hungary had protected Ukrainian Catholics from Poland and Russia, so when the Austrian archduke was assassinated in 1914, the bishop supported Austria's call to its citizens to defend their homeland. A week later, however, when Canada entered the war against Austria, he rescinded this letter, and urged complete loyalty to Canada. During World War I, despite 5000 Ukrainian immigrants being interned in Canadian concentration camps, Budka showed staunch patriotism. Still, his opponents used his first letter to attack him. In 1918, he was arrested in Saskatchewan, but the charge was dismissed. In 1919 more charges were brought in Manitoba, against which Budka insisted on defending himself. The court found "not a tittle of evidence" against him.

In 1927 ill health forced Bishop Budka to resign; his successor was the Basilian superior, Basil Ladyka. Budka returned to Lviv, which by then was under the Soviets, to act as auxiliary to Metropolitan Sheptytsky. There in 1946 he was arrested by the Stalinist regime, and died as a martyr in a Siberian concentration camp in 1949. In 2001 the church declared him blessed.

In 1948 Edmonton and Toronto became separate eparchies (dioceses), Saskatoon in 1951, and New Westminster in 1974. In 1956 Winnipeg, under Maxim Hermaniuk, was given the status of metropolitan see for all Canada. The Ukrainian Catholic Church had come far indeed.

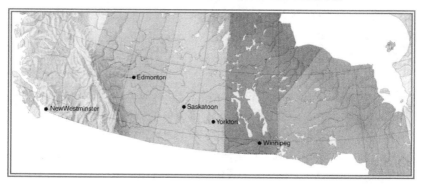

21

Language and Faith:
the Bourne – Bourassa Controversy

AFTER 1900, MASSIVE immigration, especially to the west, made new demands upon the Church in Canada. There was a need for competent personnel, although sometimes these accompanied the immigrants. For instance, the German community that settled around Muenster, Saskatchewan, after 1902 had with them both German-speaking Benedictines from Minnesota under Dom Bruno (George Doerfler), and Sisters of Saint Elizabeth from Austria under Mother Maria Pulcheria (Aloisia Wilhelm).

But funds were also necessary. For this purpose the Catholic Church Extension Society (now Catholic Missions in Canada) was founded in 1908 in Toronto; its president was Father Alfred Edward Burke (1862-1926), a priest from Charlottetown. The Society performed a vital role; for example, over the years it raised $265,000 for Bishop Budka's Ukrainian missions. However, its foundation led to real differences over language. While it had a bilingual board that included Archbishop Fergus McEvay of Toronto, Archbishop Bégin of Quebec, and Bishop

Joseph-Alfred Archambeault of Joliette, its president favoured a policy of anglicization as the only effective way to evangelize the west. Burke publicly advocated his position through the *Catholic Register*, the Society's newspaper. More from practical necessity than principle, McEvay was in agreement.

Archbishop Langevin of St. Boniface strongly opposed what he saw as an intrusion into his territory. Moreover, he regarded Extension's tendency to anglicize as undermining francophone missionary efforts in the west. Although he later relented, Langevin at first refused to accept the Society's funding. While other French-speaking bishops in the west were not of the same mind, Langevin's opposition was widely shared by the Quebec hierarchy.

Controversy intensified when at the Eucharistic Congress of 1910 in Montreal, Archbishop Francis Bourne of Westminster, England, having just finished a tour of western Canada, declared that the future of the Church in Canada would depend "upon the extent to which the power, influence, and prestige of the English language … can be definitely placed upon [its] side." He later explained that he was not excluding French, but wanted only to emphasize that without English a vast group of new Canadians would be lost to the Church. But Bourne had provoked the wrath of Henri Bourassa, editor of *Le Devoir*, who replied for French Canadians that "the best safeguard of the faith is the preservation of the language in which, for three centuries, they have adored Christ."

Within months, Bégin and Archambeault resigned from the board of Extension. McEvay was distressed; he felt that the work of the Church was being compromised by nationalist tendencies. Differences over language continued to have an effect, especially in the west, most particularly in the nomination of bishops. In 1911, on the basis that the new diocese of Regina had a plurality of French-speaking Catholics, Olivier-Elzéar Mattieu, a Quebec priest, was appointed its bishop. However, two years later, without Langevin having been consulted, the Ontario-born John Thomas McNally became the first bishop of Calgary. In 1915, just after Langevin's death, the historic diocese of St. Boniface itself was divided, and Alfred Sinnott, an Ontarian and a co-founder of Extension, was appointed Archbishop of Winnipeg.

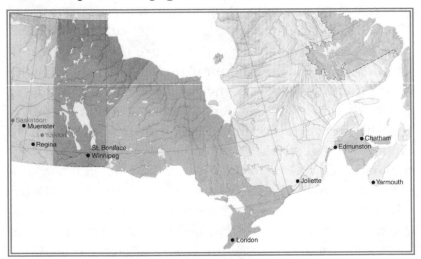

Language also led to a rearrangement of the dioceses of New Brunswick, where the largely Acadian Catholic population had no bishop of their own until the appointment of Patrice-Alexandre Chiasson as Bishop of Chatham (later Bathurst) in 1920. In 1936, however, Moncton was made an archdiocese and New Brunswick a separate ecclesiastical province, under Archbishop Arthur Melanson. In 1944, the predominantly Acadian diocese of Edmunston was created. Similar considerations led to the formation of the diocese of Yarmouth, Nova Scotia, in 1953.

Language was also an issue in Ontario, where there was a perennial fear that the Protestant majority might abolish Catholic schools. A central figure was Michael Francis Fallon, Bishop of London from 1909 to 1931. An Oblate, Fallon had been forced to resign as vice-rector of Ottawa University over language issues, and he felt strongly about them. In London, he insisted on the law that allowed bilingual, but not francophone, schools. However, his attitude was interpreted as opposition to French-language instruction, which perhaps it was, and after Bourne's remarks he was widely attacked in the French-Canadian press. Conversely, francophone Catholics in Ontario were demanding an extension of bilingual schools, and the issue divided the province's bishops. While it did not disappear, it died down considerably after the encyclical of Benedict XV, *Commissio divinitus* (1916), which deplored rivalry and suggested compromise. The scars of these language issues remained with the Church in Canada for some time to come.

22

A Nation of Missionaries: Following in the Footsteps of "Madre Bernarda"

FROM ITS BEGINNINGS the Church in Canada had a missionary character. Its earliest Catholic settlers—priests, religious, and sometimes laypersons—became in turn missionaries to both the native peoples and to European settlers in the outlying areas of the country. The Jesuits and Récollects brought the gospel from Quebec into Ontario and the Atlantic region. Later the Oblates and the secular clergy, the Grey Nuns, the Sisters of Saint Ann and others brought it across the prairies and the Rockies to the northwest coast of both Canada and the United States.

The first organized missionary activity abroad was almost accidental. In 1852, the Sisters of Providence, founded in Montreal nine years earlier by Blessed Émilie (Tavernier) Gamelin, sent five sisters to Oregon. Among these women was Sister Bernard (Vénérance Morin), who had been born in St. Henri de Lauzon, Quebec, in 1832; she had joined the congregation just two years before they set out for Oregon. In the northwest, however, the sisters met problems and decided to return to Canada. In 1853, they travelled overland to California, where they boarded a ship for home. The ship landed in Valparaiso, Chile, where the sisters found themselves penniless and ignorant of the language. However, the local population saw them as a gift from God and assigned an orphanage to their care. The Sisters of Providence accepted the new foundation as part of their mission, and sent other sisters to sustain the effort. "*Madre Bernarda,*" as she became known, established orphanages, hospitals and schools throughout Chile, and in 1880 became superior-general when a separate Chilean congregation was established (though it reunited with Canada in 1970). Awarded Chile's highest honour, the *Orden del Mérito*, in 1926, she died in 1929, aged 96. Coincidentally, Mother Joseph (Esther) Pariseau (1832-1902), a Providence Sister who went as a missionary to the northwest when the sisters returned there in 1856, and who worked incessantly for the poor, is one of the two representatives of Washington State honoured in the Statuary Hall of the United States Capitol.

Many other Canadian individuals, especially from Quebec, devoted themselves to the foreign missions. In 1869 Sister Saint-André of the Religious of Jesus and Mary became a missionary in Asia. From 1871 Canadian Sisters of Our Lady of Charity of the Good Shepherd were to be found in a number of Latin American countries, and White Sisters in Algeria from 1885. In terms of priests, it appears that Canadian Holy Cross Fathers went to Bengal as early as 1890, Friars-Minor from Canada to the Holy Land in 1898, and Canadian Jesuits to the Chinese missions after 1912.

After World War I Canadian missionary activity grew rapidly. Cardinal Bégin of Quebec was concerned to see that Canadian groups directed such efforts, and encouraged the reorganization of the Pontifical Mission Societies in Canada. This work was completed in 1922. In French Canada, a religious sister, the Venerable Mother Marie of the Holy Spirit (Délia Tétreault, 1865-1941), from Marieville, Quebec, did much to promote a missionary consciousness. In 1902 she had founded the first missionary congregation of Canadian origin, the Missionary Sisters of the Immaculate Conception. New missionary endeavours soon followed. In 1918, Father John M. Fraser,

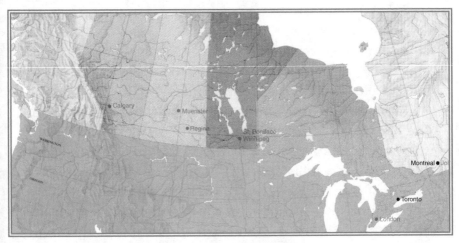

a Torontonian who went to China as a 25-year-old priest in 1902, founded the China Mission Seminary (Scarboro Missions) for secular priests from English-speaking Canada who would serve the missions abroad. In 1921 the Quebec bishops, encouraged by Mother Marie, established a parallel body, *La Société des Missions Étrangères*, at Pont-Viau near Montreal. Both groups were committed to missions in China until the Communist victory in 1949; thereafter they diversified and redirected their efforts into other countries.

In 1961 Pope John XXIII asked North America to make a real effort to provide clergy to Latin America to relieve the serious shortage of priests there. Canadian dioceses and religious congregations responded generously, and a new form of missionary activity was begun. This experience truly became a two-way street; it brought great benefits not just to the receptor countries, but also to Canada, especially in the renewal of pastoral services and a deeper awareness of social justice.

At their peak levels in 1971, Canadian missionaries abroad totaled 5256, up from 3320 in 1958. They included 21 bishops, 1548 priests, 2531 sisters, 944 brothers and 183 laypersons; the great majority, perhaps two-thirds or more, came from French Canada. Canada's missionaries were to be found in 86 countries, largely in Africa and Latin America. Canada clearly had taken to heart the courage of its first foreign missionary, the twenty-one-year-old woman who had landed destitute in Chile.

23

Practising the Gospel:
Moses Coady, Jimmy Tompkins and
Joseph Charbonneau

THROUGH ITS institutions and works of charity, the Church in Canada had consistently sought to alleviate the hardships of individuals. In the twentieth century, however, it was increasingly influenced by papal social teachings, especially those of the great encyclicals *Rerum Novarum* (1891) and *Quadragesimo Anno* (1931).

Two Canadian pioneers who tried to put such teachings into practice were Fathers Moses Coady and J.J. "Jimmy" Tompkins, both priests of the Antigonish diocese who taught at St. Francis Xavier University. Maritime fishermen and miners seemed particularly vulnerable to poverty that resulted from exploitation. In 1912, Father Tompkins developed the idea that the university should reach out to such groups through an extension program that would bring education to the masses. He managed to enlist the support of his cousin, Father Coady, and many community leaders. In 1921, the university offered its first of several "People's Schools" for 50 men and 1 woman, and in 1928 established a permanent extension department under Coady's direction.

The project underwent further development after 1922, when Tompkins was posted to Canso following a dispute with Bishop James Morrison. Observing first-hand the poverty of a remote fishing village, Tompkins encouraged local cooperation in both production and consumption: first came a lobster factory owned and operated by the fishermen themselves, then a credit union and a cooperative store. They became a model for other cooperatives throughout the Maritimes and elsewhere. In turn, cooperatives became a feature of the "Antigonish Movement" that came to symbolize such economic cooperation both in Canada and abroad.

Others were moved by different social concerns. Chief Andrew Paull (1892-1959), a Squamish from British Columbia, who had grown up on a mission reserve and who had been influenced by the Oblates, became a leader

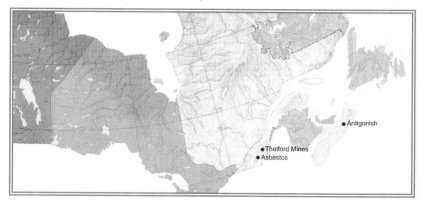

in organizing Canada's Native peoples. Locally, he promoted Native solidarity through everything from sports events to band councils, and in 1943 was a founder of the North American Indian Brotherhood, a precursor to today's Assembly of First Nations.

A defining moment for Quebec Catholicism was the Asbestos strike of 1949. The strike was a violent one, in which the Quebec government of Premier Maurice Duplessis, especially through its Provincial Police, clearly supported the company. On the other side was the Catholic labour movement, the *Confédération des travailleurs catholiques du Canada* (CTCC); through people like its secretary-general, Jean Marchand, it was influenced by the social teachings of Father Georges-Henri Lévesque of Laval University. The CTCC saw the strike as a struggle for the survival of trade unions. Duplessis considered the Catholic labour leaders *saboteurs.*

But the strikers had the support of their pastor, Father Louis-Philippe Camirand, and their bishop, Philippe-Servule Desranleau of Sherbrooke, a conservative who was led to decry the evils of capitalism. They received even stronger backing from the Archbishop of Montreal, Joseph Charbonneau. Born in Lafaivre, Ontario, in 1892, he had become Bishop of Hearst in 1939, and less than a year later was named Archbishop of Montreal. Regarding the strike, Charbonneau declared bluntly that social peace was not an absolute value, and that the human person must come before profit. "When there is a conspiracy to wipe out the working class," he said, "it is the duty of the Church to intervene." Moreover, he spearheaded a province-wide church collection that provided significant help in maintaining the strikers. Finally, after four bitter months, Archbishop Maurice Roy of Quebec, who was also sympathetic to the strikers, mediated an end to the dispute.

But the strike had important consequences. It broke the longstanding alliance in Quebec between church and state, in particular the close ties between the clergy and Duplessis' Union Nationale party. Indeed, in 1956 Fathers Gérard Dion and Louis O'Neil of Laval made a scathing attack on "*duplessisme*" and its political corruption. The strike clearly moved the Church in Quebec generally toward more liberal positions on social issues. In 1950 many of the Catholic intellectuals behind it, including Marchand, Gérard Pélletier and Pierre Elliott Trudeau, created *Cité libre*, a periodical that explored issues of social morality from a Catholic ethos but a secular and liberal ideology. The magazine became a major influence within Quebec's "Quiet Revolution" that radically changed and secularized Quebec society during the early 1960s, leading to major shifts in religious attitudes and practice.

Obviously the strike had brought Charbonneau into public and personal confrontation with Duplessis. This was certainly a factor, although perhaps not the only one, that led the Vatican to force his resignation in January, 1950, at the age of 57. Charbonneau retired to a chaplaincy in Victoria, B.C., where he died in 1959.

24

Paul-Émile Léger and Jean Vanier: Catholics in a Time of Renewal

IN 1959 Pope John XXIII astonished the Catholic world by announcing a general council. The last had been almost ninety years before, and he made it clear that this one was to be different, a council directed to the renewal of the Church, not a theological one like earlier councils.

Though Canada's bishops were undoubtedly as surprised as others, they responded faithfully with their suggestions, largely practical, and when the Second Vatican Council gathered in 1962, almost all of them were present. Canadian bishops became increasingly involved in the debates that followed, especially Archbishops Roy of Quebec, Maurice Baudoux of St. Boniface, and Hermaniuk of Winnipeg, who spoke with authority on matters regarding the Eastern churches.

The most influential Canadian at Vatican II, however, was Paul-Émile Léger, who had become Archbishop of Montreal in 1950 and was made cardinal in 1953. Léger, a Sulpician, had been born in Valleyfield, Quebec, in 1904, and was ordained in 1929. He had been a professor in France and in

Montreal, a seminary rector in Japan, and the vicar-general of the Valleyfield diocese. When he was named archbishop he was Rector of the Canadian College in Rome. Léger was a member of the key Preparatory Commission, and had considerable influence upon the Council's directions in liturgy, ecumenism, and the nature of the Church. Paul VI, who became pope in 1963, clearly respected his advice.

When the Council concluded in 1965, the Canadian bishops faced the task of implementing its reforms at home. The most immediate changes affected parish and diocesan structures, ecumenical cooperation, and worship, especially the introduction of English and French in place of Latin. There was some resistance to changes, especially when these were introduced without preparation or when treasured traditions and artifacts were discarded. Change sometimes had other unsettling effects; for example, following the Council many priests resigned their ministry, often to marry. However, the experience of the Council had a deep impact on the bishops, who faithfully promoted its reforms despite the difficulties.

The Council strengthened the Canadian Catholic Conference (renamed the Canadian Conference of Catholic Bishops in 1977), which had been founded in 1943. By bringing together anglophone and francophone bishops and those of the Eastern churches, the Conference had defused many historical tensions over language and rite. It also provided a common forum for national statements on such matters as family values and social affairs. After the Council especially, it often offered an opportunity for common action, above all with regard to liturgical renewal. Of course the Conference sometimes provoked controversy, as when it issued its statement on Pope Paul VI's 1968 encyclical *Humanae Vitae* (1968), in which the Pope had condemned artificial contraception. The bishops said that theirs was a pastoral statement intended to recall the traditional role of individual conscience, but some saw it as a dissent from papal teaching.

As a project for the Canadian centennial in 1967, the bishops established the Canadian Catholic Organization for Development and Peace to assist the underdeveloped world; in later years this organization became a major provider of aid and an important feature of church life. 1967 also saw the symbolic ending of the missionary status of the Church in Canada. Eight northern vicariates became full dioceses: Grouard-McLennan, Prince George, Whitehorse, Mackenzie-Fort Smith, Keewatin-Le Pas, Churchill-Hudson Bay, Moosonee, and Labrador-Schefferville. Some regretted, however, that the dioceses had been aligned under two archdioceses on an east-west axis, instead of recognizing the more usual north-south links.

That same year, Cardinal Léger, still only 63, resigned to become a missionary among people with leprosy in Cameroon, Africa, where he remained until 1979. He died in Montreal in 1991.

This period also deeply influenced other Canadian Catholics. In 1964, in France, Jean Vanier founded the first

L'Arche community, where those with mental handicaps could have a sense of belonging. Son of Governor-General Georges Vanier and his wife Pauline, Jean Vanier had been in the Canadian navy until 1950. He then did graduate studies, and taught philosophy at St. Michael's College, Toronto. But Vanier had been deeply touched by a visit to a small institution in France, and by the plea of the men there: "Do you love me?" In 1964, Vanier welcomed the first handicapped men to a small house in Trosly-Breuil, France and thus gave birth to the L'Arche movement. In 1968 in Ontario, he organized the first "Faith and Sharing" retreat, and in 1971, "Faith and Light communities" to assist people with disabilities and their families were born. L'Arche is now a worldwide movement, and Vanier's writings are influential, but their author has always maintained the simplicity of their purpose: to help people "grow and discover the good news of Jesus."

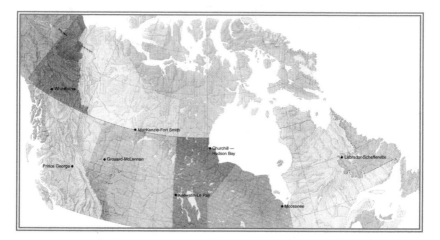

The Visits of John Paul II: Celebrating Canada's Faith

IN 1984 SOMETHING occurred that Canadian Catholics of earlier generations could hardly have imagined: a visit of the Pope. In fact, the Canadian bishops had invited John Paul II to visit Canada soon after he was elected in 1978, but his plans had to be postponed after he was shot in 1982. The 1984 papal visit to Canada was one of the most extensive made then or since—a twelve-day pilgrimage from sea to sea that touched eight provinces and the North West Territories.

After massive planning by church and civil authorities, and amid heavy security, the Pope began his visit in Quebec City on September 9. It was not merely a church event, but a national one, as the Governor-General, Madame Jeanne Sauvé, made clear in greeting the Pope as "a pilgrim of compassion and peace" whose presence underlined the spiritual dimensions necessary for human existence itself. Clearly touched, the Pope replied that his visit had two purposes: to bring to Canadians the concerns and hopes of the rest of the world, but also to bring to the world at large something of the "human energy and ... religious vitality" of Canada.

The theme for the visit, appropriately enough, was "Celebrate Our Faith." The Church in Canada was enjoying a relatively settled situation; the period of change and controversy that had followed Vatican II seemed to be past. However, neither the events themselves nor the Pope's remarks (prepared with the advice of the bishops' conference) were merely ceremonial; rather they candidly addressed the realities of the Canadian situation.

In Quebec and in Montreal, the Pope acknowledged that the traditional French-Canadian Catholic culture had been "shattered," and encouraged new efforts to inculturate the faith. In Flatrock, Newfoundland, he spoke of unemployment, and of the Christian obligation to put human needs before financial gain. At Edmonton, the Pope decried the inequities between rich and poor nations; he said flatly that the "poor South will judge the rich North." In Toronto, he noted the ecumenical spirit that characterized Canadian Christians, and re-affirmed it as "an essential part" of the Church's mission. At Yellowknife, he spoke plainly of the need for self-determination for Canada's native peoples.

The papal visit had several broad effects. It underlined the diversity of Canadian Catholicism and the widely different cultural contexts to which the Church had to be present; Canadians saw depicted a Catholic ethos that was marvellously rich and varied. It emphasized the importance to the Church of the communications media, for whatever the crowds on the ground, the remarkable television audience was so much greater; more than anything, the visit became a "television event." Finally, despite demographic variations from province to province, the visit showed that a major transition had occurred: clearly Canada as a whole no longer regarded Catholics as a minority community.

Poor weather had prevented the Pope from making a scheduled visit to the native peoples at Fort Simpson in the North West Territories. However, at his departure he promised that he would return to Canada to complete his journey. This he did in September, 1987, when after a visit to the United States he came to Edmonton and then went on to Fort Simpson.

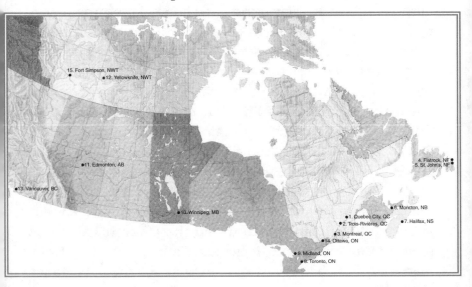

There the Pope was greeted joyously by thousands from the Dene nation and others of Canada's Aboriginal peoples. He took the occasion to address their situation even more strongly than he had done before. Reaffirming their right "to a just and equitable measure of self-government, along with a land base and adequate resources," he asked that Canada be a model for the world in upholding their dignity. Although the 1987 visit was brief, the Pope's directness had a profound impact.

At the World Youth Day celebration in Rome during the Jubilee Year 2000, Pope John Paul II promised to return to Canada once again. In response to the invitation of the Canadian bishops, he announced that Toronto would be the site for the next World Youth Day in July, 2002, and said that he looked forward to being present with the young people of the world who would gather there. On Palm Sunday, 2001, in St. Peter's Square, His Holiness entrusted the World Youth Day cross to the young people of Canada. It was to be carried in pilgrimage throughout the country to prepare for the great Toronto event.

Canadian Catholics Today:
Launching Anew into the Deep

AT THE BEGINNING of a new millennium Canadian Catholics numbered approximately 14,200,000 of about 32 million Canadians. Over 6 million of them lived in Quebec where nominally they were about 86% of the population. By contrast the Yukon had only about 6000 Catholics, even fewer than the new territory of Nunavut, and in both the Yukon and British Columbia the Catholic population was only 20% of the total. Ontario's Catholic population had grown considerably over the years, and by 2001 totalled about 4,300,000, roughly 37% of the provincial population.

Canada's Catholics belonged to 63 Latin rite dioceses, 8 eparchies of the eastern Catholic churches, and the military ordinariate; they were led by 81 serving bishops, including cardinals in Montreal and Toronto. These two dioceses were the country's largest, each with over a million and a half faithful; Quebec City had almost a million. By contrast, the smallest diocese, Moosonee in Ontario, had less than five thousand. The newest Latin-rite diocese was Rouyn-Noranda in Quebec (established in 1973), but eight northern dioceses were just six years older, and the ordinariate for military personnel had been formed only in 1986. In 1998 the number of ecclesiastical territories actually had been reduced when two in Saskatchewan were merged with others: the diocese of Gravelbourg with Regina, and the abbacy of Muenster with Saskatoon.

The ethnic background of Canadian Catholics was now considerably more varied than it had been earlier. Before World War II Canadian Catholics who were not indigenous generally had come from France, the British Isles, or Ukraine, with smaller numbers from Germany, Italy, Holland and Poland. These groups were swelled by a significant post-war immigration, especially from southern and eastern Europe, largely into southern Ontario and the Montreal region. In more recent decades new Canadian Catholics were more likely to have come from Asia, especially the Philippines, Hong Kong, Vietnam or Korea; these substantially increased the numbers of adherents in the major urban areas, notably Vancouver and Toronto.

In the last decades of the millennium the Catholic Church certainly faced serious problems. Sexual abuse scandals involving priests and brothers in native residential schools, orphanages, and parishes certainly did great harm. There was also an observable decline in traditional religious practice experienced widely throughout the country, and in the adherence of Catholics to the moral values taught by the Church. In the preceding forty years the number of priests and religious had declined, and some parts of the country faced a serious shortage of clergy. These years also saw major changes in the situation of Catholic institutions. Although this remained relatively stable in Ontario, Alberta and Saskatchewan, there had been a significant reduction of Catholic hospitals and colleges throughout the country, and constitutional amendments in 1998 and 1999 abolished the Catholic school systems in Newfoundland and Quebec.

On the other hand, the last years of the twentieth century also displayed signs of growth and hope. The renewal of Vatican II had given new life to many Canadian parishes. It had certainly involved a major re-engagement of laity in the activities of the Church, and the development of programs of adult formation. New immigrants were beginning to make their own contribution to the life of the Church, and in many areas were providing numbers of priests that alleviated the clergy shortage. Canada now had over 800 ordained permanent deacons, a recent development since the Council. Perhaps encouraged by the Pope during his visits, the Church in Canada at both the national and regional levels presented credible public positions in its teachings on marriage and the family, social justice and the rights of native peoples. It also maintained its commitment to ecumenism and dialogue with the Jewish people and other faith groups; in 1997 it became a full member of the Canadian Council of Churches.

As they celebrated the Great Jubilee of the year 2000 and prepared for World Youth Day in 2002, Canada's Catholics seemed very conscious of both the challenges that beset them and the opportunities before them. Their roots were strong and deep. Those who had gone before had passed on to them a vibrant heritage of faith. Having journeyed into the contemporary age by longboat and canoe, prairie wagon and dog team, they had also bequeathed to future generations a pioneering spirit that was not easily overwhelmed by difficulties. The combination of these two factors—faith and courage—seems particularly well suited to launch the Church into the challenges and opportunities of its second millennium.

Glossary

Archdeacon: roughly the equivalent of today's vicar-general (see below).

Beothuk: a member of an Aboriginal people formerly inhabiting Newfoundland but extinct since the early 19th century.

Capuchin: a Franciscan friar of a branch established in 1529 to re-emphasize the ideals of poverty and austerity.

Coadjutor bishop: an assistant bishop who would automatically succeed the bishop when he died or retired.

Council: an extraordinary assembly of all the bishops of the world, also known as an ecumenical council. There have been 21 ecumenical councils. The last two were the first Vatican Council (Vatican I, 1869-70) and the Second Vatican Council (Vatican II, 1962-65).

Cree: a member of the Algonquian linguistic family, with related but autonomous groups from eastern Canada to the Rocky Mountains. The Cree form the largest Aboriginal grouping in Canada.

Dene: a member of a group of Aboriginal peoples of the Athapaskan linguistic family, living especially in the Canadian north.

Donné: *see* lay associates.

Ecclesiastical province: the joining together of neighbouring dioceses by the Holy See to promote pastoral activities and foster the relations between the bishops. Such a province is headed by a Metropolitan bishop. A Metropolitan bishop is called an Archbishop.

Governor-General: The Head of State in Canada representing the Canadian Crown.

Huguenot: A French Protestant in the 16th or 17th century, especially one persecuted for his or her beliefs, or involved in civil war with the Catholic majority.

Huron: An Aboriginal group formerly living around Lake Simcoe.

Inuit: Any of several Aboriginal peoples inhabiting the Arctic coasts of Canada and Greenland. Sometimes in the past referred to as Eskimos.

Iroquois: An Aboriginal confederacy of Iroquoian peoples (originally including Cayuga, Mohawk, Oneida, Onondaga, and Seneca, and later also the Tuscarora) living in Ontario, Quebec and New York.

Jurisdiction: the power to govern such as that held by a bishop in virtue of his ordination as a bishop. Jurisdiction also refers to a place or way in which that power is used. For example, a bishop has the power of governance in his own diocese, but not in any other diocese.

Lay associates: Lay people who do not take vows but live by the spirit of the community and participate in its work.

Lower Canada (Quebec): The French speaking portion of Canada around the St. Lawrence River that is now southern Quebec.

Métis: person of mixed Aboriginal and European (often French) descent.

Metropolitan status: From meter = mother + polis = city: the principal city. An archbishop in his own diocese presides over his diocese and the ecclesiastical province suffragan to it. An archbishop's connection to the Pope is expressed in the wearing of a white stole-like vestment, called a pallium. It is made of wool with black crosses woven into it, has tabs both front and back, and is worn draped over the shoulders.

Mi'kmaq: Aboriginal peoples living in Nova Scotia, New Brunswick, Prince Edward Island and the Gaspé Peninsula.

Missions-Étrangères: A congregation of secular priests founded in Paris in 1658-1663 by Mgr Pallu, Bishop of Heliopolis, Vicar Apostolic of Tongking, and Mgr Lambert de la Motte, Bishop of Bertyus, Vicar Apostolic of Conchin-China to evangelize non-Christians and the poor.

Montagnais: A member of an Innu people living in the barrens between Hudson Bay and the Labrador coast.

Oblates of Mary Immaculate: a Roman Catholic congregation of priests and brothers founded in 1816, by Saint Eugene de Mazenod, to work among the poor and work for the renewal of a Church suffering the effects of the French Revolution.

Ojibwa: a member of an Algonquian people living especially around Lake Superior and adjacent areas. Ojibwa are found from Ontario through to Saskatchewan.

Papal Zouaves: a troop of soldiers (of whom about 400 were from French Canada) formed in Rome for the defence of the Pope, 1860-71.

Precedence: The practice of giving secular officials of rank the right of preceding others, in seating, etc.

Privy council: A body of advisors appointed by the sovereign.

Récollect: A member of the reformed branch of the Franciscan Observants, a religious order founded in France in the late 16th century.

Religious of Jesus and Mary: An order of religious women founded in 1818 at Lyon, France, by Saint Claudine Thévenet (Marie Saint-Ignace).

Residential school: a boarding school operated by the Canadian federal government and staffed by religious orders or other church personnel to accommodate Aboriginal and Inuit students.

See: the area under the authority of a bishop or archbishop (comes from the word "seat," the bishop's chair).

Squamish: a member of an Aboriginal people living in southwestern British Columbia.

Suffragan diocese: a diocese within an ecclesiastical province that is not the metropolitan diocese. Its head is a bishop who is more correctly called a suffragan bishop. He is "suffragan" to the archbishop of the province. For example, Hamilton is a suffragan diocese of Toronto.

Sulpicians: A Roman Catholic society of diocesan priests founded in Paris in 1641 and established in New France in 1657, concerned especially with the training of priests.

Ultramontane: Advocating supreme papal authority in matters of faith and discipline; advocating the subordination of the state to the Catholic Church.

Upper Canada: the mainly English-speaking region of Canada north of the Great Lakes and west of the Ottawa River, in what is now the southern portion of Ontario. It was a British colony from 1791 to 1841, when it was united with Lower Canada to form the Province of Canada.

White Sisters (Missionary Sisters of Our Lady of Africa): A religious order of women founded in 1869 at Algiers, Algeria, North Africa, by Charles M.-A.Cardinal Lavigerie, archbishop of Algiers.

Vicar: someone appointed to fulfil a particular role. A vicariate is the place in which that role is fulfilled.

Vicar-apostolic: a bishop appointed by the Pope to function in a territory that has not yet been established as a diocese. They often govern in mission territories or under adverse circumstances.

Vicar-general: an ecclesiastical officer assisting or representing a bishop in matters of jurisdiction or administration.

Vicariate apostolic: the territory governed by a vicar-apostolic.

About the Author

RAYMOND J. LAHEY, born in St. John's, Newfoundland in 1940, has been Bishop of St. George's since 1986; his residence is in Corner Brook, Newfoundland. His diocese includes L'Anse aux Meadows, the site of the first known settlement of the Vikings, North America's original Christians. Bishop Lahey studied at the University of Ottawa, the Gregorian University, Rome, and Cambridge University in England. Before his present appointment, he taught for a number of years at Memorial University of Newfoundland, where he was Professor and Head of the Department of Religious Studies. Following that he served as a pastor and vicar-general in the Archdiocese of St. John's. He has served on several commissions of the Canadian Conference of Catholic Bishops, and has been a member of the Governing Board of the Canadian Council of Churches. He is currently President of the Atlantic Episcopal Assembly and a Member of the Pontifical Council for Christian Unity. He has written previously on various historical, liturgical and theological subjects.

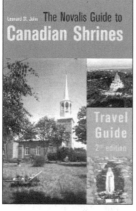

Two new Faith–building Tools

THE FAITH OF THE CATHOLIC CHURCH
Answering Your Questions About Your Faith
by *David Konstant*
Preface by *Aloysius Cardinal Ambrozic*
A user's manual to the Catholic catechism.

For clergy, teachers, catechists, youth and anyone wanting to know more about what is means to be Catholic. Here is a short, plain-language introduction to the Catechism of the Catholic Church. Organized into four parts: *The Profession of Faith • The Celebration of the Christian Mystery • Life in Christ • Christian Prayer*.

All readers will be directed "towards the maturing of their faith, putting down roots in personal life, and shining forth in personal conduct."

2-89507-260-4, 198 pages, 3⁷/₈" X 6¹/₄", $9.95

RECONCILIATION
A User's Manual   by *Fr. Michael Preur*

A *Living with Christ* resource for Catholics. The way Catholics "go to confession" has changed dramatically in recent times. Yet many who celebrate the sacrament continue to experience peace, consolation and deep healing. It is time, then, for a short, easy-to-understand summary of the theology of this sacrament – explaining its importance for all Catholics – and a how-to guide to preparing for it and participating in it. It comes into two parts: Introductory essay about the nature and purpose of reconciliation, especially the Rite of Reconciliation of Individual Penitents; and an anthology for reading, reflection and prayer used for centuries.

2-89507-166-7, 160 pages, 3⁷/₈" X 6¹/₄", $9.95

 NOVALIS *B*ook Service   Call: 1-800-387-7164
49 Front St. E., Toronto, ON M5E 1B3 Canada   Fax: 1-800-204-4140